THE PHILIPPINE BASES

THE PHILIPPINE BASES: NEGOTIATING FOR THE FUTURE
AMERICAN AND PHILIPPINE PERSPECTIVES

Fred Greene, Editor

Council on Foreign Relations
New York

COUNCIL ON FOREIGN RELATIONS BOOKS

The Council on Foreign Relations, Inc., is a nonprofit and nonpartisan organization devoted to promoting improved understanding of international affairs through the free exchange of ideas. The Council does not take any position on questions of foreign policy and has no affiliation with, and receives no funding from, the United States government.

From time to time, books and monographs written by members of the Council's research staff or visiting fellows, or commissioned by the Council, or written by an independent author with critical review contributed by a Council study or working group are published with the designation "Council on Foreign Relations Books." Any book or monograph bearing that designation is, in the judgment of the Committee on Studies of the Council's board of directors, a responsible treatment of a significant international topic worthy of presentation to the public. All statements of fact and expressions of opinion contained in Council books are, however, the sole responsibility of the author.

Copyright © 1988 by the Council on Foreign Relations, Inc.
All rights reserved.
Printed in the United States of America.

This book may not be reproduced, in whole or in part, in any form (beyond that copying permitted by Sections 107 and 108 of the U.S. Copyright Law and excerpt by reviewers for the public press), without written permission from the publishers. For information, write Publications Office, Council on Foreign Relations, Inc., 58 East 68th Street, New York, N.Y. 10021.

Library of Congress Cataloging-in-Publication Data
The Philippine bases.

   1. Military bases, American—Philippines
2. United States—Military relations—Philippines
3. Philippines—Military relations—United States
I. Greene, Fred.
UA26.P6P46 1988   355.7′09599   88-18964
ISBN 0-87609-043-9

Contents

Foreword—*William Gleysteen* and *Alan Romberg*	vii
Preface—*Haydn Williams*	xi
Maps	xiv
Part One: Issues	
Issues in U.S.–Philippine Base Negotiations	3
Fred Greene	
Possible Outcomes of Negotiations	5
A Question of Sovereignty?	6
Increased Nationalism	9
The Domestic Philippine Political Setting	11
The Timing of Negotiations	16
The Philippine Constitution	19
Military Operations at the Facilities	24
Philippine National Security	28
Philippine Vulnerability and the U.S. Commitment	34
Management of the Facilities	39
Differences over Compensation	46
Social Problems	58
ASEAN and Japan	59
Notes	66
Part Two: Conference Record	79
Part Three: Background Papers	
U.S. Facilities in the Philippines	105
Alva M. Bowen, Jr.	
The Military Bases and Postwar U.S.–Philippines Relations	130
William E. Berry, Jr.	
Members of the Council on Foreign Relations Study Group	157
Participants at the Bodega Bay Conference	158

Foreword

Over several decades, the United States has sustained a pattern of forward deployments in Asia, which has been critical to Washington's regional and global strategy of deterrence. This pattern came under strain a decade ago, in the aftermath of Vietnam. But with its system of alliances and friendly relations in the region, the United States has maintained its commitments, and its presence, relying on base facilities in Japan, Korea and the Philippines, and on various types of security and political cooperation with states ranging from Australia to the People's Republic of China and the nations of ASEAN. These arrangements have contributed to stability in the region in a variety of ways, including the fostering of a climate conducive to economic development.

At present, circumstances—including the terms of the U.S–Philippine Military Bases Agreement and developments within the Philippines—have converged to require a review of American access to facilities in the Philippines in 1988 and renegotiation of the overall arrangement before the end of 1991. Big stakes are involved for both sides. For the Philippines, questions of sovereignty, adequate compensation, and the costs and benefits of the bases for national security are at issue. For the United States, the contribution the bases make to strategic interests and to bilateral relations need to be weighed against the limits imposed by operational and budgetary requirements, anxieties over the future of the insurgency in the Philippines, concerns over corruption, and constraints on the U.S. ability to meet other demands of the Philippine side. The precedent for basing arrangements in other countries will also be of vital importance to Washington.

In order to better understand the issues and to illuminate them for the publics and governments concerned, the Council on Foreign Relations accepted with enthusiasm the proposal of The Asia Foundation Center for Asian Pacific Affairs (CAPA) to undertake a study on these questions, parallel to, but totally independent of, a similar study already planned by the Philippine Council for Foreign Relations in Manila. We were extremely fortunate to have as three of our principal participants Brent Scowcroft and Theodore L. Eliot, Jr., who served as co-chairmen of our study group, and Fred Greene of Williams College as principal researcher and author of our study. With their active assistance, we formed a study group of outstanding people from various sectors of American society to assist Professor Greene in his work and to form the core of our delegation to meet with the Philippine Council at a conference convened by CAPA. Members of the study group are listed on page 157.

Our group met formally three times during 1987, with several informal conversations between Professor Greene and members of the group throughout the year. In addition, Professor Greene traveled to the Philippines and other countries in Asia in the fall of 1986 and spring of 1987, and also paid several visits to Washington to interview officials and private citizens from various countries concerned. Although his work was importantly informed by the views of the study group members, the first article in this volume is the responsibility of Professor Greene alone.

In addition, we commissioned background papers by two acknowledged experts. The first, by Alva M. Bowen, Jr., is on the military importance of the U.S. facilities in the Philippines and possible alternatives to them. Actual implementation of alternative arrangements discussed by Bowen would be very complicated in certain respects, especially if it concerned relocation of the U.S. facilities now at Subic Bay. The second, by William E. Berry, Jr., gives some history of the bases. It should be emphasized that neither paper has been reviewed nor approved by the study group or other formal Council process. Nonetheless, we felt both papers would be of great interest to the general reader and have included them in the final section of this volume.

The Asia Foundation convened a two-day conference at Bodega Bay, California in mid-February, with delegations drawn from our Council and the Philippine Council. The views of participants from both countries were expressed as individuals, and not as representatives of either organization. Discussion was very friendly, but also quite frank. A record of the conference, agreed to by both Councils, is included as the second section of this book. A message from The Asia Foundation's President, Haydn Williams, appears as a Preface to the volume.

The Council on Foreign Relations is grateful to The Asia Foundation Center for Asian Pacific Affairs, as well as to the Philippine Council for Foreign Relations, for their initiative in undertaking this project, and

Foreword

for their cooperation in making it a success. The former is due a particular debt of gratitude for organizing funding for our Council's study. We sincerely appreciate the contribution of the Philippine Council for Foreign Relations, especially their participants at the Bodega Bay conference under the leadership of Justice Florentino P. Feliciano and the stewardship of Wilhelm G. Ortaliz, Executive Director of the Council, who coordinated the conference record with Alan Romberg.

William H. Gleysteen, Jr.
Director of Studies
Alan D. Romberg
Senior Fellow for Asia

Council on Foreign Relations
New York, May 1988

Preface

On February 15–18, 1988, The Asia Foundation Center for Asian Pacific Affairs convened a joint conference of two study groups, one from the Philippine Council for Foreign Relations in Manila and one from the Council on Foreign Relations in New York on the subject of the "U.S.–Philippine Bases Agreement: Looking to the Future." This conference at Bodega Bay, California, was the culmination of over one year's intense scrutiny of this subject independently by the two Councils' study groups.

The time is fast approaching when the Philippines will have been independent of the United States for a longer period than it was under the American flag. Colonial arrangements and attitudes are things of the past. Current economic, political, and security ties must be in accord with present realities and designed to meet the challenges of an ever-changing global environment.

Distance and historical differences between the two countries are objective factors that necessarily must be taken into consideration. At the same time, a passionate devotion to democracy and a willingness to sacrifice on its behalf are principles cherished by the peoples of the Philippines and the United States. Both these considerations are reflected in these papers, which we hope will be useful to government officials and interested citizens concerned with this subject.

The Asia Foundation Center for Asian Pacific Affairs in San Francisco works with other American and Asian organizations sharing similar goals to promote communication and strengthen understanding between the United States and the nations of Asia and the Pacific. The Foundation considers its cooperation in this important work with the Philippine Council and the New York Council to be an exemplar of Center activities.

The Asia Foundation is deeply appreciative of the efforts made by the leadership and study group members of both Councils over the past year. They have performed a major service to both countries.

Support for this project from the Rockefeller Brothers Fund, the John D. and Catherine T. MacArthur Foundation and the Corporate

Associates of The Asia Foundation is gratefully acknowledged. The supporting organizations did not participate in the preparation of these documents, and they do not necessarily reflect their views.

This report would be incomplete without my expressing appreciation for the contributions made to the success of this endeavor by the following: Theodore L. Eliot, Jr., formerly Executive Director of the Center for Asian Pacific Affairs; Edith S. Coliver, formerly Representative of The Asia Foundation in the Philippines; Herbert Levin, Diplomat in Residence and Director of Studies, Center for Asian Pacific Affairs; and Ann Devaney, Program Officer, Center for Asian Pacific Affairs.

Haydn Williams
President
The Asia Foundation

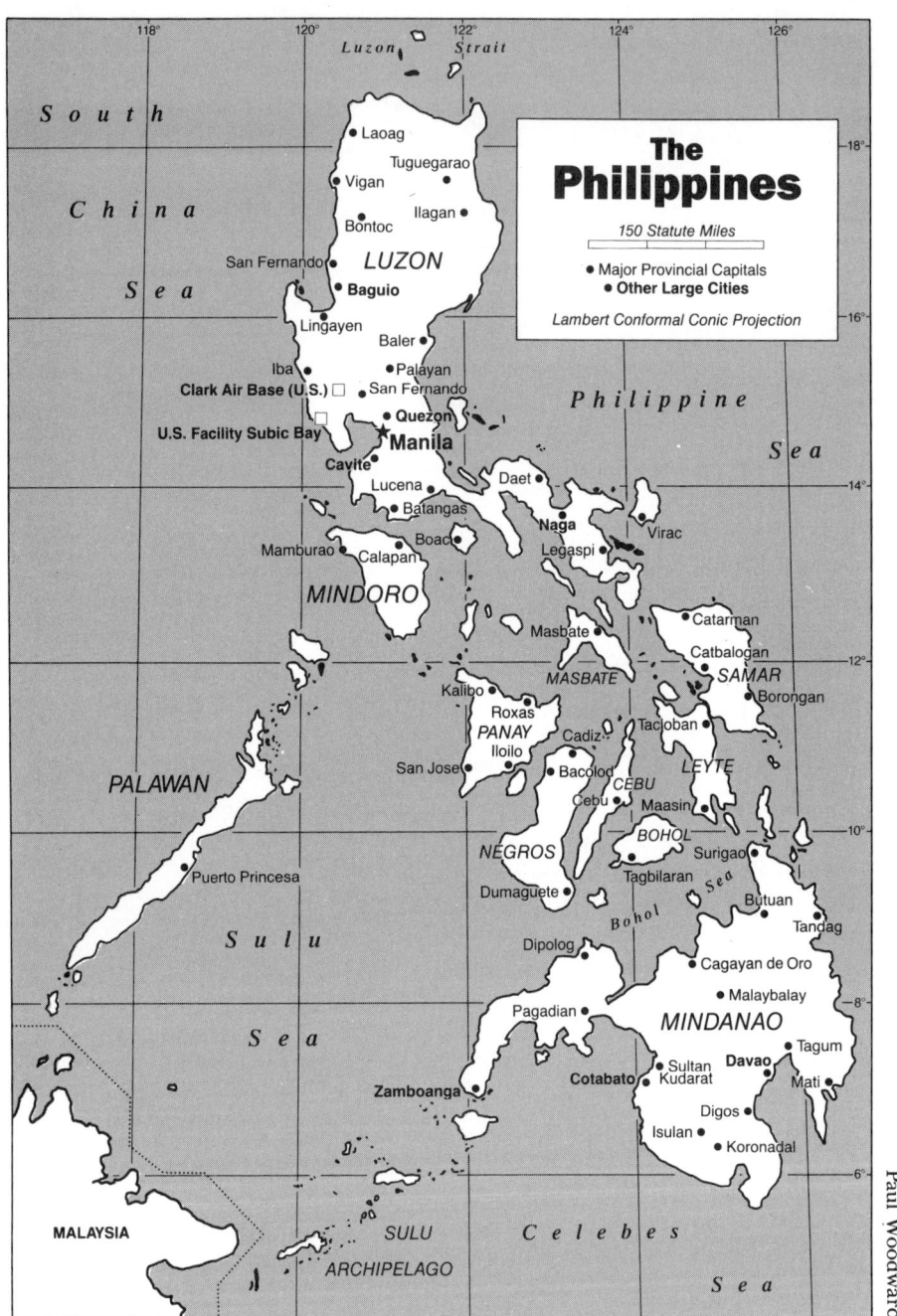

Reprinted from *Rebuilding A Nation: Philippine Challenges and U.S. Policy* (The Washington Institute Press 1987), by permission of Paul Woodward.

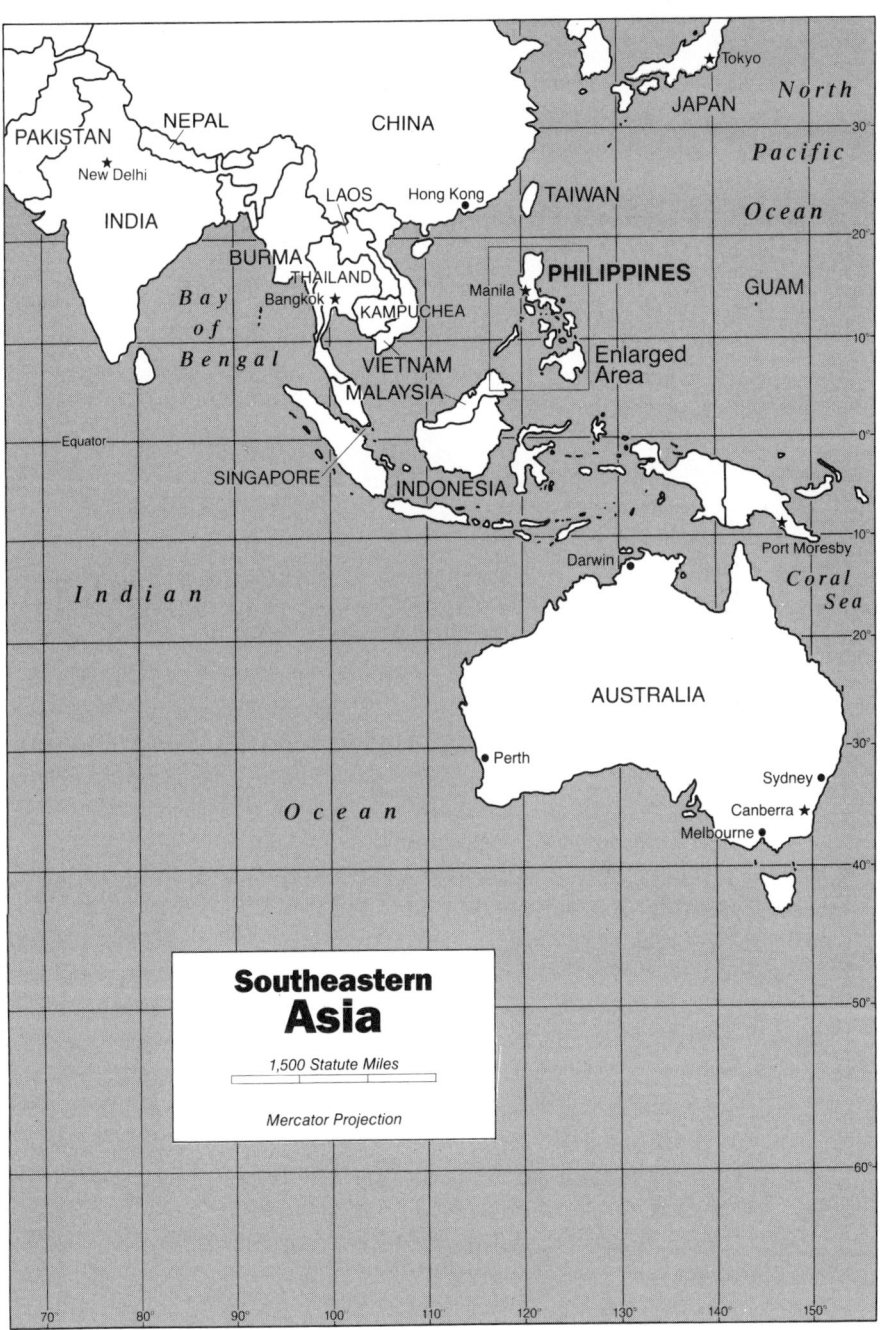

Part One

Issues in U.S.–Philippine Base Negotiations

Fred Greene

Current issues in the Philippines swirl around an ongoing struggle over the country's basic political course. After more than two decades of Marcos' rule that severely weakened all aspects of Philippine public life, the revolution of February 1986 afforded the opportunity for recovery. Corazon Aquino has proven a very popular president, carrying the voters with her in approving a new constitution, electing a new legislature, developing a new judiciary, changing tax laws, providing an investment code, and attaining a legitimacy of rule that has not existed for almost a generation. But profound difficulties remain. Economic problems continue to burden the country; the government has not yet been able to control the widespread communist insurgency or resolve the Moslem uprising in the south; it has not been able to suppress corruption or do much to foster land reform. The issues that need to be dealt with would overload the agenda of even the most determined of political leaders; the nature of Philippine politics adds to their weight. The return to a more open society has allowed a return to the rough-and-tumble political atmosphere that troubled the pre-dictatorship era. The inexperience and political diversity of the ruling coalition intensify those difficulties. In addition, the legacy of the military's distrust of the civilian government and the latter's justifiable fears of coup attempts by the armed forces put a further strain on the system.

With all these domestic difficulties, the Aquino administration would probably have preferred to put the issue of the U.S. facilities in the Philippines on the back burner. However, the five-year review system agreed to in the 1970s requires an evaluation to take place in 1988.

The review system is the result of many modifications in the original Military Bases Agreement (MBA) of 1947, which was to run for ninety-nine years, provided for no compensation, and allowed the U.S. to use sixteen facilities with access to seven more available upon request.[1] In 1966, the duration of the agreement was reduced to twenty-five years (to 1991), to continue thereafter subject to one year's notice of abrogation by either party. In the mid-1970s negotiations began on the provision of compensation, with $500 million for five years agreed upon in 1979, followed in 1983 by $900 million for the next five years. The number of facilities used by the U.S. was sharply reduced over the years, so that today there are only two major installations at Clark Field and Subic Bay, plus three smaller ones and one site for rest and recreation.[2] The revision of 1979 also provided for five-year periodic reviews. Since the first was concluded in 1983, the next review comes due in 1988, just three years before the completion of the fixed term in 1991.

For the Philippines, negotiation over the U.S. facilities is of major importance. A successful outcome—that is, one satisfactory to both parties—could have a most beneficial effect on Philippine stability and the country's prospects for sustaining its new democratic system. Washington, too, has a significant stake in reaching an acceptable accommodation, not only because the facilities are of strategic importance, but also because it is in the U.S. interest to see the issue resolved in a way that enhances and strengthens Philippine stability and democracy. Nevertheless, it is likely that the Philippines will exert great pressure for major changes that will severely tax the U.S. ability to reach accommodation.[3] Given its own requirements and constraints, Washington faces a challenging period of negotiation.

It is the purpose of this paper to examine the issues that are likely to arise between the U.S. and the Philippines in the negotiations over the future of the facilities after 1991. In addition to considering likely U.S. attitudes and positions, the paper will consider Philippine objections to the current arrangements, as well as basic Philippine attitudes that will influence the negotiations.

From the often divergent U.S. and Philippine perspectives, the analysis will consider Philippine constitutional stipulations requiring a treaty prohibiting nuclear weapons, control over base operations, security of the Philippines, the problem of compensation and questions of the timing of discussions during the 1988–91 period. These matters must be considered in the context of Philippine feelings about matters of sovereignty, the rise of Philippine nationalism, and the current political situation.[4]

Possible Outcomes of Negotiations

The negotiations may lead to a *variety of possible outcomes.*

1. The greatest degree of continuity, of course, would result from *agreement under which U.S. forces would remain* at Clark and Subic into the 1990s, albeit with a number of modifications in the arrangements. This would require resolution of the treaty and nuclear issues, understandings over control of operations at the facilities, and settlement of questions of compensation. Each of these topics is quite complex and presents many different possible resolutions. They are all closely interrelated, and the selection of an option in one area may have an impact on the range of choices in the others. For example, the level of compensation will likely be related to the nature and duration of a post-1991 accord as well as to the degree of U.S. control over the funds. It is therefore fairly difficult to project outcomes.
2. *A qualitative change in the current arrangements* could well result from the very wide differences that separate Washington and Manila regarding compensation, Philippine insistence on greater sovereign control, and American requirements for considerable freedom of operation. A qualitative change could take the form of retaining some facilities at reduced levels, with lease-back for other parts, especially at Subic and perhaps Clark, with emphasis on repair and maintenance work and logistical support. This might be done in conjunction with a dispersal of some activities to other locations in Southeast Asia and elsewhere. A change in arrangements about the facilities would inevitably affect the level of U.S. compensation to the Philippines and consequently its support for Philippine development and democracy.
3. Should the two parties fail to reach an accord on even a reduced presence, *the U.S. would have to depart* from Philippine bases. To minimize the bilateral and regional impact of such an outcome,

there could be an extended phase-out, with installations gradually turned over to the Philippines. A combination of new facilities could be put into place in Guam and other islands to the east. Additional possibilities include western Australia, some Southeast Asian countries, and a port facility in Japan. The U.S. could still achieve many of its strategic objectives under this new dispensation[5], although it is more expensive and markedly less desirable than the present arrangement, particularly with regard to Subic Bay. The increased costs could, however, prompt fundamental questioning of the U.S. forward policy in Asia. In addition, resentments generated by a failed effort to reach agreement could impinge upon subsequent cooperation and affect U.S. attitudes toward the continuation of the 1951 Mutual Defense Treaty (MDT).

With these three possible major outcomes in mind and recognizing that the U.S. strongly favors the first—retention of the facilities at Subic and Clark—it is important to consider the specific issues in the negotiations. Beginning with increased Philippine nationalism and Manila's domestic political setting, the paper will address:

- the timing of negotiations
- the Philippine Constitution
- military operations at the facilities
- Philippine national security concerns
- management of the facilities
- compensation
- social problems.

It will conclude with some observations on the regional setting in which these negotiations will take place.

A Question of Sovereignty?

Foreign bases are seldom popular in any country, especially among the political elites sensitive to issues of nationalism and sovereignty. They are likely to be critical and unappreciative of American efforts to take account of local sensitivities. Attitudes in the Philippines are no exception.

An upsurge of Philippine nationalism has resulted in the determination to assert sovereign rights over the U.S. base facilities, and it underlies much of Philippine thinking on the base issue. Many Filipinos look upon the facilities as a vestige of colonial rule, imposed on the country as a price for its freedom and an arrangement that flawed its independence from the outset. Indeed many argue that the country is so permeated by American culture that it is still struggling to find its own identity after more than four decades of self-rule.[6] A large and continuous American presence simply prolongs the dilemma. Some foreign ministry officials, in particular, who are clearly influenced by the attitude of Third World countries toward the Philippines, wish to see the Philippines more clearly accepted as a "non-aligned" country.[7] The bases, however, obviously hamper this acceptance; the Philippines has never been able to attain better than observer status at non-aligned meetings.[8]

Some foreign ministry officials argue that the very existence of the bases causes a great psychological dependence on the U.S., and that, even if the U.S. facilities remain, greater sovereign control over them would be an important positive step.[9]

There is similar widespread sentiment among Filipino elites that, despite the concessions made over the past three decades, the base arrangement is still unfair. One veteran Philippine diplomat describes the modifications as repairing only half the problem.[10] Many consider the original 1947 arrangements as so bad that only a brand new deal could rectify what they perceive as an enduring and unfair historical legacy. This historical infirmity, they feel, must be repaired and changed to conform with current realities and to eliminate vestiges of extraterritoriality. From an American perspective, major concessions—as noted below—have radically changed the original agreement into one that is balanced and equitable. Thus, there is a deep issue here, with Philippine negotiators seeking to have the U.S. treat the remaining issues on their terms.[11] There is also widespread resentment expressed by Filipinos that the U.S. poses as a generous friend, yet behaves niggardly and offers "too little, too late".

Finally, many Filipinos believe that the U.S. intervenes in Philippine affairs and exercises too much control over the country's political process.[12] They continue to make an issue of Washington's identification with and support of President Marcos until almost the end of his regime. They still rankle over statements by Vice President Bush in 1981 and President Reagan in February 1986, interpreted in the Philippines as asserting the primacy of the bases over democracy among American interests.

There is concern that U.S. aid to the Philippines, with its requirements for detailed American supervision, is not only a derogation of economic sovereignty but is a means for the U.S. Congress to exert substantial influence over Philippine politics. Even though the current leaders found U.S. pressure acceptable when it was applied against the Marcos regime, American influence on domestic Philippine politics deeply offends local sensibilities. There is ongoing concern over potential U.S. engagement in Manila's struggle against the insurgents, even though current policy limits cooperation in military training.[13] But the willingness to suspect U.S. intervention was manifest in the rumors that American officers and facilities were involved in the abortive coup attempt of August 28, 1987.[14] In fact, the U.S. embassy in Manila, through its military officers, forcefully warned Philippine military officials that all aid would be cut off should the army overthrow the Aquino government. This position was later reiterated by the commander of U.S. forces in the Pacific, Admiral Ronald Hays.[15]

Questions of sovereignty permeate many of the specific issues and intensify the difficulties in resolving them. Each major substantive problem, with its own long history of disagreements and compromises, becomes harder to handle when associated with concerns over sovereignty. To cite some of the major issues thus affected (all of which are discussed later in greater detail):

1. *Base Agreement.* To satisfy sovereign pride and a need for dignity and equality, the Philippine government has required in its new constitution that there be a new agreement and that it be adopted by both sides in treaty form. The U.S. government has always treated this arrangement as an executive agreement, does not wish to be instructed on how to arrange future accords, and is not eager to establish an undesirable precedent for negotiations elsewhere. Further, there could be serious problems for a treaty in a U.S. Senate ratification process.

2. *Compensation.* Philippine officials are expected to seek significantly higher compensation in any multiyear arrangement, to be paid regularly in set amounts and free of all restrictions.[16] American officials believe that the U.S. has honored its overall commitments and that American congressional powers over funds cannot be preempted. Arguments abound over the use of the term

"rent," a label desired by Manila and strongly resisted by Washington. In addition, American officials see little or no chance of Congress approving uncontrolled disbursements of any sizable magnitude, especially when corruption in the Philippines is perceived to be an as-yet unresolved problem.
3. *Operational Control.* Philippine officials seek increased control over base operations to square with their perceptions of national interest and security.[17] U.S. officials hold that they require operational freedom, and some feel the U.S. has yielded too much control already, for example, in the area of base perimeter security. (In fact joint patrols were resumed after the murder of three Americans near Clark Air Base in October 1987.)
4. *Nuclear Weapons.* On several past occasions, Philippine negotiators have pressed for an absolute ban on the storage or presence of nuclear weapons and delivery systems on their territory. While making important concessions (e.g. to consult on the matter of deploying land-based missiles), the U.S. has adamantly stood by its worldwide policy of neither confirming nor denying (NCND) nuclear deployments as a general principle essential to its global security responsibilities.
5. *Criminal Jurisdiction.* Philippine officials seek to extend, at least nominally, their primacy in criminal jurisdiction over U.S. military personnel. Americans complain of already significant extensions of Philippine authority and look for relief on several counts.
6. *Defense Commitments.* Critics in Manila find the U.S. defense commitment inadequate and lacking the "automatic" aspects of America's NATO obligations. They also resent what they perceive as their own inability to keep from becoming entangled in America's international quarrels. U.S. officials, however, consider the MDT commitment, which came four years after the 1947 MBA, binding on the U.S. and have reasserted this on many occasions. They point out that the large force presence assures Philippine security to an extent Manila could not possibly achieve on its own.

Increased Nationalism

Philippine nationalism is by no means a recent phenomenon in a country that resented Spanish rule and fought a bitter three-year war of independence against the U.S. at the turn of the century. During the negotiations for Commonwealth status and complete independence, competing political leaders invoked nationalist sentiment against their domestic rivals as well as against the U.S. Similar arguments were made during efforts to revise the MBA over the following decades. While the ultranationalist and leftist critics of the bases were generally small in number, they were vehement in their opposition, keeping pressure on the government to make extensive demands.[18] Even the Marcos administration, which posed generally as close to the U.S., stimulated ultranationalist sentiment in order to pressure Washington for better terms. Marcos' opponents were fiercely anti-base, seeing them, and the associated assistance since 1979, as helping to maintain him in office.

The same nationalist sentiment prevails today, perhaps even intensified by the more open political system that enables critics to influence the bargaining process significantly.

Anti-American feeling runs more deeply among the young than the old, especially at institutions of higher education attended by children of the well-to-do elites. Many in the younger generation, along with their teachers, are hostile to U.S. multinational corporations, to U.S. economic relations, and to the U.S. security link. In particular, they consider the bases as both the cause and essence of the dependency relationship with the U.S. Many regard the U.S. presence as antithetical to nation-building and to the achievement of democracy, economic development, and social justice. They feel that the U.S. supports the exploitative Filipino overlords while it prevents other domestic leaders from pursuing national development by making them subservient to and dependent upon a foreign power.

American businessmen in the Philippines have observed a rise in nationalism among the business community, which is becoming increasingly hostile toward foreign investors, whose superiority in technology, money, and organization breed resentment.[19] In fact, restrictive nationalist laws have long curtailed direct foreign investment, despite the country's need for foreign capital.

There are various strands of nationalist positions on the bases. There are ultranationalists, heirs to Senator Claro Recto, who oppose the bases on principles of national interest, dignity, and autonomy and do not wish to bargain. They view the bases as illegal entities that should not even have been mentioned in the constitution. Another, less adamant, nationalist position recognizes that the facilities serve Philippine as well as U.S. interests (and even see the validity of some U.S. requirements). However, they view previous arrangements as so one-sided that they would allow them to remain only if the U.S. yielded to extensive demands. Finally, many "pragmatic nationalists" are willing to bargain from a less rigid position and accept an arrangement that gains significant concessions, following good-faith give-and-take bargaining that adequately recognizes Philippine sensibilities.[20] Despite their moderation, these people believe they need important U.S. concessions both because they are justified and to blunt the appeal of the anti-base ultras.

A convergence of factors makes Philippine nationalism particularly strident and politically potent at this time: the new democratic government that includes many pre-1986 anti-base and anti-Marcos leaders; the 1991 deadline; and the belief that this is the country's first real crack at renegotiating the bases arrangement as an independent nation-state. But the ultranationalists do not enjoy overwhelming support and, in fact, considerable moderation still characterizes the position of many leaders. Some of them recognize privately if not publicly that the Philippine government now enjoys real leverage that should not be thrown away by refusing at the outset to have U.S. facilities beyond 1991, or by rigidly insisting on extremist terms. Instead, they wish to settle the major issues on favorable terms, in return for which they would see that the bases are removed as an issue of national contention (much as Japan did after 1960). Given the wide gap presently separating the Philippine and American positions on specific points, and the tumultuous nature of current Philippine politics, this will require a high degree of statesmanship in both governments.[21]

The Domestic Philippine Political Setting

The Philippine domestic scene is characterized by a public generally supportive of retaining U.S. bases and an opposition that sets the terms of the confrontation and debate.

Frequent polling indicates consistent support for retention of the U.S. facilities with substantial majorities (2:1 or better). The public as a whole still values the relationship with the U.S. Large numbers of Filipinos have close relatives in the U.S. and many still wish to emigrate. To many, the bases remain a symbol of U.S. interest in their country and they would view an American departure with concern. In fact, the proportion in favor has risen since the February 1986 revolution, after a modest decline in the late Marcos years.[22] In the area around the bases where employment is a major positive consideration, support is quite strong, and American analysts believe that the insurgent Communist forces refrained from attacking Americans—until October 1987—in good part because the U.S. presence is such an important source of income.[23] There is, however, the widespread belief among opponents that most people support the retention of the bases because they are unaware of the specific issues involved in the negotiations. (In fact, almost half the Philippine population is unaware that the facilities even exist.[24])

Critics of the American presence vow to launch what they call an education campaign to turn the tide in their favor. In the present democratic environment, a vigorous free press has begun to produce a steady stream of critical pieces, particularly in the metropolitan Manila area, where 15 percent of the country's population lives. These articles include references to social problems (drugs, AIDS, smuggling, and prostitution); emphasis on the danger that the bases allegedly pose as a magnet for nuclear attack; and claims of U.S. intervention in Philippine politics. Like the country's no-holds-barred political tradition, the media have engaged in what their critics describe as irresponsible behavior.[25] Opponents of the bases have also criticized American efforts to publicize the economic and other benefits derived from the bases, which, they argue, "inadvertently foster a divided loyalty" and have the effect of creating a popular constituency for the MBA.[26] The same might be said for well-publicized medical aid programs such as the *Mercy* hospital ship visits to ports, which have treated over 100,000 people.

The articulate and determined opposition has dominated the debate, overshadowing discussion of the positive dimensions of the American military presence. When security aspects are discussed, especially by the Anti-Base Coalition (an umbrella organization of more than 100 cause-oriented groups organized in 1983), it is in advocacy of non-alignment, support for ASEAN's Zone of Peace, Freedom and Neutrality (ZOPFAN), and stress on a Southeast Asian nuclear-free zone. Rarely does the debate focus on the country's external security needs or issues of broader regional security.

At a higher political level, there has been an absence of enthusiasm for openly backing continuation of the base arrangements, a condition that has guaranteed the initiative in the debate to the opponents. Apart from a few military and civilian strategic analysts, most public officials give the impression of merely tolerating the facilities or, at best, maintain a low profile. As a result, if there is no change, the political climate between Washington and Manila may deteriorate steadily over the next few years. Negative developments (like a halving of U. S. military aid to the Philippines for FY 1987, which Congress later restored), can seriously impair an already tenuous position. If the political climate worsens, and if Philippine leaders believe that the U.S. repeatedly lets them down, the prospects for a successful renegotiation may become imperiled. At the same time, if Filipinos are unwilling to acknowledge effective American steps, this too will sour the atmosphere.

The passivity of the government and the strength of the opponents were reflected in the actions of the Constitutional Commission in 1986. The commission, appointed by the president, included vocal and well-organized critics of the bases who advocated restrictive anti-nuclear terminology as well as a provision essentially requiring that the MBA be terminated in 1991, to be replaced by a new treaty. The government did not become involved in the commission's deliberations and allowed matters to drift until finally devising a limited escape route on the nuclear issue. Those commissioners who struggled to protect what they perceived to be a position in support of Philippine-U.S. relations felt battle-scarred from their bruising encounter with those who sought immediate abrogation of the MBA. Thus, with a determined opposition still holding the initiative, a favorable outcome for the MBA is by no means assured, despite a generally supportive public.

Over the next four years, the actions of President Aquino will be pivotal. Given her strong showing in the presidential election of February 1986, her capacity to gain overwhelming support for the constitution a year later, and the victory of twenty-two of twenty-four candidates on her slate in the Senate elections in May 1987, her reputation for carrying the voters on major decisions remains impressive. Even the series of coup attempts and questions about Mrs. Aquino's leadership style have not yet undermined her popularity or the aura of legitimacy surrounding her office and that of the political system that she has put into place. Thus far the president continues to hold the key to negotiations over the facilities and—assuming that her power and influence do not slip in the interim—she should be able to sustain her position with the Senate and in a referendum, if one is held.

President Aquino has indicated that she sees the U.S. as supportive of her position and seems amenable to retaining facilities, subject to adequate compensation and modifications that take into account Philippine sensibilities about sovereignty. Her task, then, is to use her bargaining leverage in the negotiations that lie ahead with the U.S., as well as with those at home who oppose any renewal.

The challenge for the U.S. is to help her sustain her political strength while asserting its position on the difficult substantive issues that will surface in the upcoming negotiation. The U.S. has bolstered the Philippines with economic assistance above the level promised in 1983, with support for Manila's request for loans from international agencies, with bilateral trade preferences, and with backing in its efforts to reschedule bank debts.[27] Yet Philippine need is so great, and hopes were so high (because of strong assurances of support from U.S. officials after Aquino's victory), that a huge gap exists between Philippine expectations and the actual U.S. performance since the restoration of democracy. Nonetheless, further increases will be hard to come by, given the current U.S. budget squeeze.

Because of economic strains, the stress of Philippine politics, and the unavoidable diminution of influence as the 1992 date for the end of her term approaches, Mrs. Aquino's dominant position is likely to erode. As noted, her "party" encompasses a wide spectrum of views, and many of her supporters oppose a new bases arrangement.[28] With an unwieldy coalition that is difficult to manage, decision-making becomes slow and uncertain, a condition that will intensify as others jockey to succeed her. Even if the executive branch becomes more coherent and unified, the legislature may still try to assert its strength, making use of the separation of powers embodied in the new constitution.

The Philippine Senate plays a pivotal role in the drama over the bases, since it has the power of ratification, and could even become directly involved in the negotiating process itself. Toward this end a Senate subcommittee was set up in September 1987 to study the U.S.–Philippine base agreement. As many as six senators may seek the presidency in 1992, a fact that could affect how they position themselves. With eight or nine senators on record with anti-base positions and only eight or nine votes needed to block ratification, an uncertain climate already exists in that body.[29] Senate President Jovito Salonga, who in the past advocated ending the MBA, is well versed in the issues;

his ability to control the debate and its schedule could complicate matters further. Much depends on how loyally he supports President Aquino's approach to the negotiations over the next few years.

Indications of Aquino's influence were evident during the legislative election campaign early in 1987, when anti-base senatorial candidates on the Aquino slate dropped their plans to run on a platform of terminating the MBA in 1991. Instead, her slate agreed to support her pledge to keep options open on the future of the bases after 1991.[30] Mrs. Aquino's strategy kept the base issue from further complicating her already difficult efforts to get increased U.S. economic support. This kind of delicate situation will persist, since the Philippines will be seeking substantial help in aid, trade, and debt relief for the foreseeable future.

A final complication in Philippine senatorial and presidential politics is the calendar—with notice of abrogation or a new arrangement due in 1991, followed by legislative and executive elections in 1992. If the government gets an arrangement to its liking in 1991 and needs but a few swing votes in the Senate to reach the total required for approval, it could induce the Senate to approve the plan and then, with both houses agreeing, put the matter up to a referendum as the constitution allows. Legislative support for a referendum would follow the tradition established in the 1930s of having the public decide such a weighty matter. This would also allow the legislators to avoid accusations of corruption that often accompany such a critical vote as well as sharing political responsibility for a highly politicized issue. If, however, the Senate blocks the treaty and there is no referendum, the 1992 campaign, in which all Senate seats are to be contested, could focus on this single issue. The arrangement might be salvaged by the election of more pro-base Senators in June 1992 (before the one year abrogation notice is completed in September 1992).*

* According to the American interpretation, the termination "clock" starts no earlier than September 16, 1991. Treaties and other International Agreements Series (TIAS) 6084 states "Unless terminated earlier by mutual agreement of the two governments, this agreement and agreed revisions thereof shall remain in force for a period of twenty-five years from September 16, 1966 after which, unless extended for a longer period by mutual agreement, it shall become subject to termination upon one year's notice by either government."

The Timing of Negotiations

Clearly, questions of timing in the negotiations become important and have an impact on substantive issues. The 1979 agreement provided for review of the MBA every five years; the next review is due in 1988. However, since the Philippine consensus holds that the agreement *expires* in 1991 and must be replaced by a new treaty or arrangement, two questions arise: how to conduct a review that covers only a three-year terminal period, and when to enter into the major renegotiation whose completion by 1991 is implicitly mandated under the Philippine Constitution.

Many Philippine experts argue that termination notice may be given in 1990, to take effect in 1991. Indeed, they argue, the MBA language permits it and the Philippine Constitution requires it. Under such a scenario, the ratification decision would rest with the current Philippine Senate, without any possible intervention by the one elected in 1992.

A strong case can be made for keeping the 1988 review brief, limited as to subject matter, and distinct from the fundamental base renegotiation talks that could begin a year or two later. A persuasive argument, however, can also be made for the opposite position—that the 1988 talks should merge into the more basic renegotiation, that channels once opened should be extended procedurally and substantively, and that an agreement to terminate, extend, or replace the MBA be reached as soon as possible.

Arguments for Keeping the 1988 Review Limited

With a relatively new government, and with massive challenges for national security and the Philippine economy, as well as for institution building, the administration would lack time to prepare for an extensive review in 1988. A limited review would give it time to develop its position on the complex issues that will mark the later renegotiation of the MBA. The government could also use the time to test the political waters at home, since open debate rather than secrecy is predominant in this post-Marcos era. The very active and outspoken media will play a major role, as will the Philippine Senate. Even if Washington and Manila agree on a limited agenda in 1988, and even if not at the table, the Philippine Senate will play a role in the 1988 review process. Further, with a U.S. presidential election in 1988, it may appear to Manila that a limited review, centering on a compensation package for

1988-91, is the sensible course to follow. It could then move into more extensive negotiations in 1989, after the new U.S. administration settles in.

From the American perspective, this approach also has attractions. A comprehensive review in 1988 makes little sense just before the U.S. presidential election and the onset of a major MBA renegotiation. The Philippine need for more time to develop its full negotiating position adds to the value of keeping the 1988 agenda limited. Moreover, a full-scale review of an arrangement that may have no legal standing after 1991 or 1992 makes little sense.

Arguments for a Comprehensive 1988 Review

However, an early start on the major issues could also prove beneficial to both parties. Several experts on both sides have noted that, except in 1983, past negotiations have been protracted and difficult, and at times had to be adjourned and resumed at a later date.[31] The overall time frame (1988-91) is relatively short, and unanticipated delays or obstacles have a way of cropping up with disturbing frequency. The schedule of political elections is so crowded that this consideration alone could jeopardize the effort unless substantial work were done early. The U.S. election of 1988, as noted, could put off serious new talks until the latter half of 1989, leaving only two years in which to complete the task. Then, with both U.S. and Philippine elections due in 1992, the MBA could easily become victim of these campaigns if negotiations had not advanced substantially by 1991. A recession in the U.S., which could give rise to strong protectionist sentiment as well as even lower aid programs, might also occur in the near future. An early start to the negotiations could minimize the impact of such developments as well as provide a better indication to both sides of what the possibilities of agreement may be.

An early start might also help in dealing with the U.S. Congress. A good beginning to the discussion would improve prospects for a larger financial package during the interim 1988-91 period. This assistance, in turn, could benefit the overall negotiation by creating a favorable climate in which to consider the major issues. More generally, it must also be realized that the U.S. Congress, like its Philippine counterpart, must be involved in the negotiations from the outset; a bipartisan consensus and a minimum of surprise are prerequisites for the legislative support required to implement any agreement. (Despite the intervening U.S. congressional elections of 1988 and 1990, most members of Congress tend to win re-election and would still be in office throughout this period.)

Early progress would also benefit both parties if it took place before President Aquino approaches the end of her term in office. While the idea of keeping options open as long as possible does enable the Aquino government to gain time and develop its negotiating position, many Philippine experts believe that a simple deferment without positive negotiations can create a harmful political vacuum, one that invites pressure groups (both U.S. and Philippine) to pre-empt or influence the policy process. Such actions and appeals to public opinion over the heads of constituted authorities could, it is feared, lead to bitter and divisive disputes. Given the complexity of the issues and the great stakes involved, there is a strong case to be made for confidential soundings and diplomatic probing at the outset, and for reaching understandings as early as 1990 or the beginning of 1991.

A 1988 Review Leading to Major Renegotiation?

A compromise position would be to conduct a limited review in 1988 but to keep the existing process and negotiating channels essentially intact upon its completion and to move directly into discussion of the MBA itself. This arrangement would induce Philippine officials to clarify their own position at an early date, to gauge American reactions, and to learn of U.S. plans. The earlier the negotiations start, the greater the chances for reducing problems and maximizing prospects for completion of an accord by 1991. Alternatively, if the talks should fail, early indications of U.S. plans for moving out or making other adjustments would enable Manila and Washington to minimize dislocations in handling these contingencies.

U.S. officials may find value in a continuing dialogue that sustains the channels opened in 1988 but may still wish to keep the review and the renegotiation separate, since any accord reached under the 1988 review can cover only three years. However, U.S. officials would probably discuss details if their Philippine counterparts brought them up, in order to identify them precisely, establish the positions of the two parties, and seek possible common ground. Procedurally, this low-key approach would not lead to substantive agreements or understandings in the 1988 review but could set the framework for formal consideration of the issues after its conclusion.

The duration of a new agreement also raises tangled questions. All Filipinos state that any agreement must be "temporary," but this does not mean that they are committed to a future of short duration. It could, for example, mean acceptance of a U.S. presence without a specific termination date—so long as the sovereign power to end the relationship rests in the hands of each signatory. Thus an indefinite continuation is a possibility, with provision for abrogation on one year's notice, as in the present agreement. However, despite the pressures this might create for abrogation on short notice, if Philippine negotiators seek a compensation package of five year's duration, the U.S. might insist upon an arrangement that also lasted at least five years.[32]

Moreover, from a U.S. military perspective, a minimum extension of ten years might be required in order to justify the investment in major repairs that will be needed to upgrade the facilities. Indeed, to undertake significant new construction might require a twenty-year arrangement. It remains to be seen whether an extension of one or two decades—with provision for subsequent abrogation—would provide an acceptable basis for agreement if this arrangement also included provisions for review every five years.[33]

The Philippine Constitution

There are two important statements in the 1986 constitution related to the U.S. military presence in the Philippines: Article XVIII (Transitory Provisions), Section 25 regarding the facilities, and Article II (Declaration of Principles and State Policies), Section 8 concerning nuclear weapons.[34] They state:

> Art. XVIII Sec. 25. After the expiration in 1991 of the Agreement between the Republic of the Philippines and the United States of America concerning Military Bases, foreign military bases, troops, or facilities shall not be allowed in the Philippines except under a treaty duly concurred in by the Senate and, when the Congress so requires, ratified by a majority of the votes cast by the people in a national referendum held for that purpose, and recognized as a treaty by the other contracting State.
>
> Art. II Sec. 8. The Philippines, consistent with the national interest, adopts and pursues a policy of freedom from nuclear weapons in its territory.

Filipinos are very proud of the constitution that they drafted to reflect and celebrate the triumphant return of democracy. In the plebiscite of February 1987, the overwhelming endorsement of the constitution further enhanced the legitimacy of the Aquino presidency, since she campaigned vigorously for a strong affirmative vote to validate her own position as well as the fundamental structure of the new political order[35]. Manila will not amend the constitution in order to meet U.S. requirements. Filipinos recall with anger the Bell Act of 1946 (which expired in 1974) that required a Philippine constitutional revision before the U.S. would give compensation for the country's war losses. They also seem to have discounted the negative reaction in the U.S. against the Philippines' having enacted in its constitution a requirement that the U.S. negotiate a treaty.[36]

The Treaty Clause. The 48-person Constitutional Commission (Con Com) that drafted the constitution had a solid group of 16 anti-base members. The Con Com Committee that considered the base question was dominated by opponents; the first resolution, with 17 signatures, called for dismantling the facilities and prohibited nuclear-armed vessels in Philippine waters. It was opposed, even by some who were against the bases, on the grounds that such a harsh measure would fail in a plebiscite and could well bring forth strong American retaliation. The opponents brought up New Zealand—which has banned all nuclear-armed or nuclear-propelled vessels from entering its waters or visiting its ports—as their model, but critics noted the sharp American reaction in suspending security obligations to New Zealand, even with no facilities at stake. The next hostile resolution, to dismantle the facilities by 1991–92, passed the base committee but suffered a 29–15 defeat in the Con Com as a whole, after a vigorous debate in which many members publicly supported the bases for the first time. There followed a 26–15 vote for the more moderate compromise clause that gained adoption. It was set among the transitory provisions, indicating an intent to settle this matter in the near future and not treat the bases as a perpetual issue.

While keeping the outcome open, the clause did require Philippine Senate ratification of a post-1991 arrangement by a two-thirds majority and stipulated that the agreement had to be "recognized as a treaty by the other contracting State." Further, as noted, it stated that the MBA would "expire" in 1991—in contradiction to the language in the agreement. Finally, while some urged that a referendum be mandatory, the decision was to make this an option if both houses so decided, following senatorial ratification of the accord. (More recently some Filipinos have suggested that the referendum might precede Senate consideration of the agreement.)

One of the most telling arguments used by the victors in the final Con Com vote centered on Manila's opportunity to strike a new deal, now that it had real negotiating leverage for the first time. Arguing they had couched the clause so as to maximize the country's bargaining position by requiring a new arrangement and in treaty form, the victors pressed for leaving all other aspects of the negotiation open for the president rather than have the constitution restrict her freedom of action.

Much has been made since the summer of 1986 about the usefulness of this leverage to improve the compensation arrangements, yet this motivation did not surface in the original Con Com debates. Instead they focused on the legal-juridical aspects of sovereignty, national equality, and the need to sweep away the onerous record of the past. The Philippine drafters found it particularly troubling that their Senate had ratified the 1947 MBA, and all amendments as far as 1965, as treaties, whereas the U.S. treated them as executive agreements.

Opponents of retaining the facilities had the additional tactical motive of making a future arrangement more difficult by requiring three steps to enable any negotiated settlement to come into force: Philippine Senate approval by a two-thirds vote, a referendum (likely to occur, even if optional) and perhaps U.S. Senate approval, also by a two-thirds vote. These opponents may make adherence to this process, especially a formal U.S. treaty ratification, a major political issue in the hope of making it all but impossible for the government to deviate from this difficult course.

Even those who favor a successful new agreement argue that Philippine and American senatorial approval guarantees the legitimacy of the accord and safeguards Philippine sovereignty. They recognize the difficulties inherent in the American treaty ratification process but want the matter considered in a manner parallel with the Philippine process.

Obtaining greater funding in a new arrangement may not have been an original motive for Philippine constitutional stipulations, but it has now become a major issue. Both diplomatic and defense officials in the Philippines have long argued that American aid has been insufficient, unreliable, and too tightly controlled. They see in a treaty obligation, which would include arrangements for compensation, improved prospects on all these counts: a treaty, they believe, would comprise a solemn American obligation. Present funding reflects merely a "best effort" promise by President Carter in 1979 and President Reagan in 1983 to seek over a five-year period certain sums ($500 million and $900 million respectively) from the Congress. Under the new setup, Filipinos believe the money would be guaranteed, and the U.S. Congress could not affront Philippine sovereign dignity by either earmarking sums (e.g. as between economic or military aid) or adjusting the totals each year.

The Philippine position would require that the treaty include all crucial funding decisions (totals, annual amounts, categories, duration, etc.), so that a U.S. Senate ratification then binds the U.S. Congress to its terms. Some Filipinos even argue that an annual appropriation below agreed-upon levels would be tantamount to a treaty violation, allowing the Philippines to repudiate the pact. Others, who do not seek abrogation under such a rigid set of requirements, nonetheless talk of terminating the treaty if one of the contracting parties generally fails to live up to the basic agreement, after allowing some good-faith leeway in this matter.

The U.S. position is sharply at odds with the Philippine treaty requirement as well as with the linkage of such an accord to specific sums and their timely delivery. U.S. officials consider it unprecedented—and unacceptable—that one state should unilaterally stipulate in its constitution the method by which another party should put a bilateral agreement into effect. Nor do American officials agree with the Philippine constitutional interpretation that, as matters now stand, the MBA is automatically terminated as of 1991, since the 1966 agreement allows it to go beyond that date (subject to one year's notice of termination). Even more unusual is the proposal that a treaty should stipulate funding, a process that the U.S. Congress is most unlikely to accept.

Beyond that, it is highly improbable that the Congress would agree to a multiyear appropriation of security assistance, since it has not done so in support of any base agreement in recent years. Even when a treaty obligation requires funding, as in the case of the United Nations, the U.S. has kept the option to reduce funds or hold up payment when conditions—such as waste at the UN—were deemed to warrant such drastic measures.[37] Moreover, as an American constitutional and political issue, the Senate cannot obligate the House of Representatives, which originates money bills, on future expenditures. For these reasons the U.S. has adhered to "best effort" pledges in all such arrangements, and these have (albeit grudgingly) been accepted by other states.

In general, the U.S. opposes the idea of formally earmarking specific amounts of assistance money for base or access agreements. The current non-specific, best-effort linkage fits in with the American view that security assistance* should more appropriately be viewed as serving the common defense interests of both states. Particularly troublesome is the view that shortfalls could call the validity of an agreement into question.[38] The U.S. seems likely to oppose the idea of a treaty—or executive agreement—that stipulates monetary commitments on grounds of law, national policy, and fear of setting an undesirable precedent.[39]

There is also the practical consideration that an executive agreement, the form in which all U.S. arrangements for operational base facilities are concluded, is a lot easier to put into effect. This is the case even when Congress becomes involved in negotiating and implementing an executive agreement. As experience with the Panama Canal and SALT II treaties of the late 1970s indicates, passage with a two-thirds majority in the Senate can be problematical (the first barely getting the necessary 67 votes and the second never even coming to a vote). The Senate can also add very difficult specifics to an accord—and has frequently done so in the past—as a price for passage.

Further, the Supreme Court in the past has treated an executive agreement as the equivalent of a treaty.[40] Therefore, the Philippines could consider that, by following this procedure, the U.S. has "recognized as a treaty" any such arrangement. Thus far, however, the Philippine position has remained firm that a formal treaty process is required of the U.S. for any post-1991 arrangement. Filipinos often cite the case of Spain, whose negotiations with the U.S. they follow closely,[41] because Madrid gained a base treaty in 1970. However, this was preceded by an executive agreement in 1963 and served as a bridge to ultimate Spanish membership in NATO. More importantly, it was superseded by an executive agreement on base use concluded between the U.S. and Spain in 1983.[42] Some people have suggested that a deadlock might be avoided by an explicit American statement that an executive agreement is the "equivalent" of a treaty.

* "Security assistance" encompasses both strictly military aid and "economic support funds" (ESF).

The nuclear clause. On the surface the constitution appears to provide a straightforward ban on the presence of nuclear weapons in the Philippines, either on land or in its territorial waters. Some of the constitutional commissioners made just this claim when explaining the constitution at meetings held before the popular vote in February 1987 on its ratification. These speakers, however, stressed the qualifying phrase "consistent with the national interest" as indicating that the government could make an exception for defense and security reasons.[43] In fact, a formal resolution unanimously adopted at the Con Com stated that the nuclear prohibition was *subject to* the national interest and that the government could therefore make exceptions in this regard.

Still, the ideal of a nuclear-free Philippines is stated in the constitution, and the government has come under constant pressure from antinuclear activists to follow this interpretation and so keep out U.S. aircraft carriers and other nuclear-capable ships, unless certified not to be carrying nuclear weapons. Leftist demonstrators have demanded that the clause be strictly enforced or that a stricter provision be enacted.[44] Former Defense Minister Enrile has repeatedly held that the constitution, taken literally, forbids nuclear weapons and that it should be amended by plebiscite to allow greater flexibility in a more straightforward manner.[45]

The vulnerability of the government's position—asserting its flexibility through the national interest loophole—is reflected in legislative efforts to pass bills "implementing" the nuclear provisions of the constitution by an outright ban on all nuclear weapons. Such bills were in fact introduced in the Senate in August 1987.[46] (See page 26.)

Article 8 is an attractive target for politicians and anti-base activists who will wish to force the government's hand on this issue in determining exactly what the constitution means, and so undermine U.S.-Philippine security relations.[47] Thus, despite the formal resolution in the Con Com allowing the president leeway, the issue is far from settled[48]. Some hope for resolution is found in the fact that satisfactory formulations and arrangements have been worked out in other countries where similar problems existed.[49]

Military Operations at the Facilities

The sensitive question of nuclear weapons at Clark and Subic is part of the broader issue of U.S. autonomy in operating the facilities. The greater the autonomy, the more the Philippine leaders can argue that their sovereignty is directly impaired. The current arrangement gives the U.S. crucial rights of unrestricted access and unhampered use of the facilities. Such unimpeded operational flexibility covers transit to and from the country and movement between facilities in the Philippines. Ships and planes can come and go freely. The U.S. also has unrestricted use of designated areas for training, including the right to use live ammunition. Further, it has the right to use roads and electricity to the extent deemed necessary in emergencies or crises. Thus, the Americans control their own operations, logistics, and maintenance.

While the U.S. has made adjustments to Philippine sensitivities, it has endeavored to keep as much operational freedom as possible. The commitment to engage in prior consultations before placing long-range missiles at the facilities remains in effect, as does the commitment to consult before using the facilities to engage directly in military combat operations abroad—apart from those conducted in implementing the U.S.–Philippine Mutual Defense Treaty of 1951 and the Manila Pact of 1954. These two commitments, both made in 1959, were explicitly reaffirmed in the 1983 review. (Language in the intervening 1979 review on unhampered military operations—specifically with respect to unobstructed movement of ships and planes—had raised concern that these commitments to consult had been impaired.[50])

In addition, the U.S. has informally promised not to use the installations for offensive actions against other ASEAN states or against Japan. The U.S. was even more self-limiting in not using the facilities to launch air attacks on North Vietnam during the 1965–73 period, a policy that one Filipino observed must have been galling as well as costly to the U.S., which then unexpectedly had to operate from Guam.[51]

The Philippine position on overall operational controls, however, is one of considerable dissatisfaction with present arrangements. In the abortive 1976 negotiations, Manila presented 25 positions that some Philippine Foreign Ministry officials today say are still very much part of their government's agenda.[52] These 1976 points included (1) the requirement that the Philippines approve all military combat operations that project American power abroad; (2) an absolute prohibition on all nuclear weapons in Philippine waters as well as on land; (3) a prohibition on nuclear-powered vessels entering Philippine waters; (4) prior Philippine approval of any third-country use of the facilities; and

(5) Philippine right to take over the operation of the installations in a national security emergency.

Consultation. On the first point, the Philippines wish to expand the American consultation commitment to include Philippine veto power over American power projection abroad, an arrangement that Filipinos feel would validate their claim to real sovereign control.[53] To officials in Manila, a commitment merely to consult confers no legal capacity on the Philippines to block an activity that its government believes is not consistent with its own national interest. Though the U.S. has in effect committed itself not to use its forces in the Philippines for attack in Southeast Asia, again there is no legal barrier that Manila can cite if it wishes to prevent such action. The possibility of U.S. forces based in the Philippines becoming involved in combat in the Persian Gulf or the Middle East is frequently cited as a way in which the country could become embroiled in an armed conflict from which it would like to distance itself. In the case of the Middle East, relations with the Islamic world, access to oil, and identification with other Third World countries are reasons for dismay over any such development.[54]

U.S. officials would oppose having its military operations depend on authorization from the Philippine government. In their view, combat operations might be required during a war or a crisis in which the need for Philippine approval could delay or inhibit action thereby endangering American lives and interests.

Nuclear Weapons. As noted, the nuclear issue is already on the table, with two bills filed in the Philippine Senate in August 1987 to ban nuclear weapons from the country.[55] They were filed by ten senators, not including Senate President Salonga. These bills, currently held in committee, would ban storage of nuclear weapons, visits by nuclear-armed aircraft or vessels, or entry even by nuclear-powered ships not bearing nuclear arms. In this respect, they follow closely the position taken by the Philippine negotiators in 1976.[56] Whereas some of the bills' sponsors are anti-base, others have not focused on the connection between a nuclear-free policy and the issue of retaining the facilities. Still other senators do not necessarily oppose continuation of the U.S. presence but view the measures as leverage for President Aquino during the MBA negotiations. There seems to be little grasp of the crucial global aspects of the U.S. policy of NCND, a failure that has caused other American allies in Asia considerable dismay.

Third-Country Access. Less salient than the prior consultation and nuclear issues, but nettlesome nonetheless, is the matter of third-country access to and use of the facilities.[57] As a sovereign country the Philippines seeks the power of prior approval for the U.S. to allow aircraft and vessels of third countries to use the facilities. Though not listed among the 25 issues remaining from 1976, it was in the Philippine draft proposal of that year and remains another issue of Philippine sovereign rights.

Singapore has had small air detachments of F5s and A4s training routinely at Clark Field in a publicly acknowledged but low-key way. Thai and Korean contingents also come for training exercises. In the past, there were multilateral activities that included Australia, New Zealand, and Thailand, but all training now is on a bilateral basis. Japanese naval vessels also come to Subic Bay during their worldwide training cruises. For reasons of national sovereignty, the Philippines wants all U.S. arrangements to remain bilateral, but with each one contingent upon Manila's approval.

As matters now stand, third-country visits are determined by the U.S., subject only to Philippine customs and immigration control. Many Philippine officials, therefore, do not see Clark and Subic as truly Philippine bases, despite the presence of a Philippine flag and commander, with Americans presumably having the status of guests. Though visits by other Asian forces may make the facilities more palatable to Philippine politicians by symbolically sharing the burden of the U.S. presence, the visitors prefer to deal directly with the U.S., to engage in high-tech realistic bilateral training with the Americans, and to keep Philippine involvement at its present minimal level. Philippine officials not only see this as a politically unacceptable arrangement, they also feel that the visitors are benefiting unfairly by not paying enough for the use of the facilities. This further complication makes for even more difficult bargaining.

Intelligence Operations. Philippine negotiators in the past have also complained about inadequate exchange of intelligence with the U.S.; in 1976 they sought a full sharing of all intelligence gathered at the facilities.[58] Sensitive Philippine nationalists are disturbed that the 1983 arrangement denied them access to areas "where classified equipment or information is located" except "in accordance with mutually agreed procedures."[59] U.S. security requirements would allow little leeway for concessions or access to these facilities. However, the two parties do exchange a considerable amount of information, the Filipinos providing data on their internal security situation and the U.S. on the situation in Asia.

It is difficult to find a firm basis for compromise on the sensitive issues related to the military operation of the facilities. Could an expansion of informal American commitments on prior consultation, which are already more extensive than the formal arrangements, provide a framework for accommodation? Could a balance be struck by a commitment to resolve nuclear issues "in a manner acceptable to both countries," with implementation of arrangements to be worked out so as to be consistent with both NCND policy and Philippine sovereignty? As for tactical activities at the facilities, is it possible for the U.S. to retain essentially unrestricted operational flexibility but, within that framework, be able to satisfy the Philippines with expanded joint exercises, some civilian Philippine air presence at Clark Field, and broader commercial use of the Subic Bay area with adequate security controls? Could a viable arrangement on the third-country question give the Philippines more of a say in determining access without impairing the effectiveness of this arrangement? And, would more detailed provision of information on conditions abroad that could pose threats to Philippine external security satisfy Manila's requirements regarding intelligence?

Philippine National Security

A series of important issues on how the facilities relate to Philippine national security reflects markedly different perceptions in Washington and Manila. Official U.S. analysts see Clark and Subic as contributing significantly to the protection of the Philippines against external threat, as well as to global and regional deterrence. Many in Manila minimize prospects of an outside threat and argue that the U.S. presence increases the Philippines' risk of entanglement in foreign conflicts, especially the risk of a possible nuclear attack against the facilities. The two sides are also at odds over the extent and reliability of the U.S. commitment to defend the Philippines under the MDT.

Many Filipinos observe that since no foreign threat confronts their country today, there is no national security need for the facilities. In contrast to the 1950s when there may have been a danger of invasion, they believe that internal insurgency presents the fundamental challenge to security. They give the impression that their insular orientation is so pronounced that they simply have not examined security questions at the regional or global level.

The political struggle at home, the nation's economic difficulties, and the challenge of the insurgency have reinforced a natural tendency to view matters primarily in a bilateral manner—whether dealing with the U.S., Japan, the Sabah question, or the country's role in ASEAN. The absence of a NATO-like support structure in Asia reinforces this one-on-one atmosphere, making the U.S.–Philippine relationship especially vulnerable to negative comments, such as: "The facilities are of no use in dealing with the insurgency"; "They do not prevent, but rather encourage, the expansion of Soviet influence in the region"; and "They might not even be of much help in case of invasion."

An even more nationalist stance holds that if the Philippines should ask the U.S. to leave, it could still retain security benefits as the French did when they withdrew from the military arm of NATO after 1968. Since, in their view, other states in the region would agree to host the U.S. forces (out of fear of the Soviet Union and to receive more aid), the Philippines would still be protected, but at a much lower cost.

However, the likelihood is that the U.S. would move eastward to areas under its own control, rather than westward to another country where it might encounter problems similar to those in the Philippines. In that case, there would be no forward shield, as there was in the case of France. Moreover, the New Zealand experience should reinforce this concern, for while that country evidently assumed a continued U.S. defense commitment after banning visits by nuclear-powered or -armed vessels, it instead faced the loss of close defense ties with the U.S., which left many New Zealanders feeling less secure than they did before the break.[60]

U.S. officials of course have a very different view of the value of the American presence, not only for the direct defense of Philippine territory but also to protect that country's broader security interests, including its sea lanes and other lines of communication in all directions. Americans, however, have found it very difficult to convince their counterparts, outside the Philippine military, of these contributions based on a "real world situation." They see the Filipinos as unable to evaluate their security situation, in part because the orientation is so alien to traditional perceptions in Manila. Further, this argument arouses suspicions that the Americans are seeking to lower the price for the facilities by claiming this "added value." For their part, Americans suspect that Filipinos claim that the facilities are of far greater value to the U.S.—or serve only American security interests—as a way of reinforcing demands for greater compensation.

From a regional perspective, some Southeast Asian and Japanese experts hope that with the new political order in place and the base issue coming to the fore, the Philippines might now be in a position to rethink its overall situation. They argue that it is time for the Filipinos to consider how important the bases are to the stability of Southeast Asia, to the entire western Pacific, and therefore to the security of the Philippines as well.

For their part, Filipinos have traditionally maintained that the bases serve essentially U.S. strategic purposes and afford a security umbrella for ASEAN's non-aligned states, but only peripherally do they provide security for the Philippines.[61] When he became foreign secretary in October 1987, Raul Manglapus called upon ASEAN to "adopt" the bases because, in his view, the member states believe that the facilities enhance regional security.[62] (Japan has also been urged to offer declaratory support to alleviate Manila's burden, as well as aid trade and investment to help rebuild the Philippine economy.[63])

An adjustment of Philippine orientation in the direction sought by its neighbors may have begun to be realized in President Aquino's welcoming statement to the other ASEAN heads of government at the summit meeting in Manila on December 14, 1987. She touched on the theme that her country was further removed and therefore more secure from an external threat than the other ASEAN states. More important, however, she went on to emphasize her sense of "strong responsibility for maintaining peace and stability in the region and beyond." In this context, she noted the country's "major role in keeping an equilibrium among the great powers in Southeast Asia, perhaps in the entire Asia Pacific region." In particular, she stressed the Philippine contribution "to the securing of the airspace and sea bases that are vital to . . . our neighbors in Southeast Asia, East Asia and the Pacific." The Philippine president thus implied a willingness to help sustain the region's security while restating her belief that this undertaking went well beyond the Philippines' own immediate national defense needs.[64]

In recent years the base facilities have been described with increasing frequency as posing a danger to Philippine security by entangling the country in a war not of its own making. Most dangerous would be involvement in a superpower confrontation in a distant land where a local war might lead to a significant escalation.[65] Americans respond by emphasizing both the remoteness of a danger arising from so distant an encounter, and the deterrence value of the bases in preventing its outbreak in the first place. In the event that there were a global conflagration, Americans argue, every nation, with or without bases, would be severely affected. Thus the key to security is deterrence, not avoidance. The U.S. also argues that the requirement to consult before deploying forces directly into combat, as well as the record of American sensitivity to Philippine concerns, is ample proof that extreme actions would not be taken in disregard of Philippine vital interests.

The danger posed by the facilities as a nuclear magnet—that is, a target of a Soviet strategic strike—has become the most potent argument to rally public opposition to the bases. Polls at the end of 1986 showed an overall opposition to the U.S. facilities of only 20 percent, but about two-thirds of that (or 14 percent of the total) attributed this to the nuclear danger (with the other 6 percent stressing considerations of sovereignty). Basically, these Filipinos assume a Soviet attack against such prime targets as Clark and Subic is inevitable in a nuclear war. They point to numerous studies that estimate the damage and conclude that the risk of having the American presence is therefore unacceptable.[66] From this perspective, there is little appeal in the contribution of the bases to deterrence. Instead of affording protection, they are depicted by those who oppose extending the agreement as increasing the prospects for a Soviet blow.[67]

This "magnet theory" is fed in good part by the ASEAN doctrine of ZOPFAN and by recent Indonesian and Malaysian efforts to create a nuclear-free zone in the region. It has also been reinforced by visiting Australian academic and church groups who are vigorously engaged in anti-nuclear activities, and by the worldwide anti-nuclear campaign in general, as well as by the absence of any serious consideration of deterrence. The possibility that the superpowers would engage in a limited nuclear exchange rather than in a suicidal all-out war has been cited as making the Philippines more likely than the U.S. to suffer a nuclear strike. The fact that the Soviets have only a limited military capability at Cam Ranh Bay in Vietnam is used to reinforce this point—by asserting that Moscow would use these modest and vulnerable assets precisely to launch such a limited nuclear strike at the outset of hostilities.

The counterargument centers on the strength and durability of the doctrine of deterrence. Philippine and other military officials and defense scholars contend that the powerful U.S. presence in itself wards off the threat of attack. From a global perspective, the argument is that the worldwide interdependence of American and allied facilities holds the key to effective deterrence; it comprises both the price and the benefit of a genuinely mutual security system.

U.S. bases around the world have, to date, not been directly threatened, and there is no reason to suppose that Clark and Subic would be singled out for special treatment. Considerable doubt also exists about whether a surgical strike, or a limited nuclear war, is even plausible. Both the U.S. and the Soviet Union have stressed that the prospect of escalation is crucial to the credibility of deterrence. Beyond this, even some Filipinos agree, other targets in East Asia would have equal or higher priority than the Philippine facilities. In a major crisis, Northeast Asia would be pivotal, with Southeast Asia playing a secondary role. For its part, Singapore assumes that some of the visiting American ships may bear nuclear arms, making that port a target too, but that a war would destroy all in any event. Military bases are not the only magnets or even the most important ones; industrial areas are at least as likely to be hit.

Moreover, if the U.S. installations were abandoned, the Soviets might still assume an American return in a time of crisis. Because of the central location of the Philippines, a major contestant would either try to fill any power vacuum there or seek to deny its use to a rival. Given Philippine weakness and the importance of the locale, even professions of neutrality might be to no avail.

Thus, it can be held, a surgical and limited nuclear strike targeted on U.S. forces in the Philippines does not seem a credible prospect.[68] These arguments have not been made forcefully in the Philippine public arena, though they may receive more attention in the next few years. Thus far the anti-nuclear case has had a much more effective public airing.

The issue of a nuclear threat is a highly emotional one and the disagreements over this matter will not be easily resolved.[69] Less intense than disagreements over the nuclear threat but also divisive is the issue of the Soviet presence in Vietnam and the balance between the superpowers in Southeast Asia. One argument for a continued U.S. presence in the Philippines is the rise of Soviet naval and air power throughout East Asia, including Cam Ranh Bay. Whatever the formalities of the arrangement between Moscow and Hanoi, for all practical purposes the Soviets have created a permanent base of operations there with hardened facilities, underground fuel supplies, and at least seven piers (where the U.S. had two). However, opponents of the American presence turn the point around with the argument that the Soviets came to Southeast Asia only because the Americans were there, in order to establish a regional balance of forces. Therefore, they say, it follows that both parties should be induced to leave, returning the area to a much lower level of tension. They cite Gorbachev's July 28, 1986 Vladivostok speech implying such a trade-off, and even more explicit statements later on, in support of this case.[70]

The American argument is that the Soviets do not respond merely to an American presence but develop plans over a long period according to broader national objectives. Thus from 1975 until the early 1980s, the U.S. reduced its presence in Southeast Asia but the Soviets kept building their forces. Moreover, during the 1970s, the Soviets established a series of naval bases in Southwest Asia when there was no U.S. naval presence to speak of, as they took advantage of political opportunities in South Yemen, Somalia (briefly), and then Ethiopia. Gorbachev's implied offer notwithstanding, therefore, an American departure or significant drawdown of force might not induce the Soviet Union to respond in kind. The Cam Ranh Bay facility enables Moscow to strengthen its credentials as a world power, enhances its position in dealing with China, allows its ships to stay on station in the Indian Ocean and the Persian Gulf for shorter periods, and gives Vietnam reassurance of Soviet support against possible Chinese threats.

So, there is no doubt that a presence at Cam Ranh Bay has raised the Soviet threat capacity in the region.[71] Nonetheless, the facilities are of limited war-fighting importance and do not compare in the global strategic balance with the U.S. presence in the Philippines. In particular, U.S. naval power at Subic dominates the nearby area and the Indian Ocean, and remains the controlling factor in both the peacetime balance and in time of crisis.[72] Consequently, a trade-off would require the U.S. to yield a pivotal strategic position in return for the Soviet evacuation of what is, despite its advantages, at most a peripheral facility.

Philippine Vulnerability and the U.S. Commitment

Although a majority of the Philippine population, including the interested elites, see no imminent security threat to their country, a case can be made that external security requirements do exist, and that the U.S. facilities play a needed, if unappreciated, role. There is some benefit derived just from the existence of security ties and the knowledge that the two countries have a close relationship. Clearly the U.S. is committed to support the Philippines in a crisis situation. If not now, then in the future, this fact would help deter challenges that might otherwise plague a country suffering from such a limited capacity to defend itself against foreign pressures.

On the other hand, the U.S. is perceived throughout Southeast Asia as having backed away from South Vietnam in its moment of crisis, and it is believed that the U.S. Congress, which played a major role in that decision, could insist on a similar course in the Philippines. Americans themselves recall their inability to protect the islands in 1941–42 and understand such Philippine concern. The Soviets might be expected to play upon these and other fears in a future crisis in order to drive Manila toward a neutralist stand. The American argument is that the historical relationship, the formal treaty commitment, the strategic importance of the facilities, and the presence of such a substantial combat presence all demonstrate that the U.S. possesses the means as well as the will to defend the Philippines, just as it is locked into the security of South Korea and Japan.

It is also argued in some East Asian countries that the close security association with the U.S. enhances the international prestige of the Philippines and raises its importance in the region. Rather than hurting the country's standing in the eyes of its non-aligned neighbors, the American connection is claimed to give it some leverage in dealing with ASEAN, Japan and even China—in part because these states see benefits to their own security stemming from the American presence on Luzon. Whatever the merits of this argument, it carries little weight in the Philippines. Opponents of the bases stress that the link to the U.S. keeps the country from becoming a solidly accepted member of the non-aligned world.

For those Philippine analysts who acknowledge that the country has national defense requirements, even if no external threats are immediately apparent, there is uncertainty about the focus of security concerns. Defense officials tend to view Moscow as the primary long-term problem. They cite the Soviet presence at Cam Ranh Bay, Soviet overflights of Philippine waters, offshore patrols by Soviet submarines, and the general projection of Soviet power in the area. They have begun to factor the Soviet presence into their defense calculations because a threat from this source is always possible.[73] The concern of the Philippine military leaders over Soviet power reinforces their commitment to the U.S. facilities. However, as noted earlier, those hostile to the American presence are convinced that this Soviet activity occurs because of the U.S. facilities.

The public at large is unclear about the identity of the external threat to the country. To many, the Soviet problem does not loom as large as potential danger from the major East Asian states, China and Japan. It is recalled that in 1975, President Ferdinand Marcos in his visit to China observed that the two countries were a "mere ocean apart."[74] Today, unresolved issues still remain, including potentially disruptive territorial disputes in the South China Sea, especially following the discovery of energy deposits. These have become more active again, recently, with fighting between China and Vietnam in the Spratleys. The anti-Japanese element remains very strong more than four decades after the Second World War. Analysts in other Southeast Asian states note that anti-Japanese feelings run much deeper among Filipinos than elsewhere in the region. This manifests itself in Manila's ambivalence over Japanese investment in the country and its deep suspicions about Japanese rearmament.

Finally, Vietnam arouses some concern because of its relative power in comparison with its Southeast Asian neighbors, as well as because of its occupation of Cambodia and the problems that generates for regional stability and the security of Thailand. Hanoi's close links to Moscow upsets Filipinos, as does its domestic policy that spawns a flow of refugees to the Philippines and other lands. There is also a suspicion that Vietnam sends some arms to the Communist New People's Army, whose insurgency Manila has still not been able to bring under control.

In sum, there is considerable appreciation of the need to consider external security problems, but only among a small minority. Articulation of the specific issues remains somewhat rudimentary, and there is no consensus on either the near-term or long-range nature of such threats. This leaves the Philippines a long way from concurring in the

American appraisal that protection against the Soviet Union should be the top priority in the external security field.

The lack of an external defense capability makes it difficult for the Philippine government clearly to identify long-term threats or to explain how it would deal with them. By assuming much of the country's external security task, the U.S. presence enables the Philippine armed forces to devote its entire effort to counterinsurgency operations,[75] and even here, it is the American naval presence that affords the country some coastal protection.

At present, Manila has no meaningful capability for defense against an external attack. It could be said that the Philippine leadership is wise to drop expensive projects, as in cutting back on the navy and in concentrating on helicopters rather than fixed-wing aircraft. After all, the country is poor, and battling the insurgency must take priority. But defense officials also believe that the nation should eventually develop forces for external security, yet this is now further from realization than it has been for decades.

The Philippine navy is very small, in poor repair, and with inadequate maintenance facilities; the few small craft in service do not provide even a credible coast guard function. The aspiration for a "blue water" navy is at present completely beyond the country's reach. The air force has a few modern combat planes, but these are grounded for lack of ammunition, training and maintenance. It has helicopters, but, again, the more advanced types are too difficult to maintain. With 7,000 islands, the country needs a vast number of helicopters that even the U.S. cannot supply in the necessary quantities and that the Philippines probably could not absorb. It might take as much as $2 billion for the country to develop a force capable of protecting sovereign air space, without even considering follow-on annual costs of operation.

The army is in better shape than the other two services, at least in terms of personnel, but it sorely lacks mobility, command, control, and communication facilities, adequate ammunition and other supplies, and the money required for sufficient training. The U.S. has for years hosted Philippine officers in training programs, but when they return to their homeland they find their soldiers without pay, supplies, training, or vehicles and barely living off the land. Twenty years of graft and corruption under the Marcos regime resulted in severely diminished U.S. military assistance. It will take years—and billions of dollars—

before the new leadership can significantly improve the limited military capacity of its forces.[76]*

Finally, it should be noted that the inability of the Philippines to provide for its own air defense poses a serious problem for the U.S. In addition to a lack of airpower, Philippine radars do not work with sufficient reliability. The U.S. has therefore provided radar screen and tactical air defense support to the country, a fact much appreciated by the Philippine military but not recognized by the public at large.[77] The U.S. also does long-range air patrolling at sea, with Philippine liaison. Admittedly, much of this activity is to monitor the Soviet presence, which Philippine officials generally consider to be an American problem rather than their own. Still the U.S. does not want to shoulder this responsibility alone as part of a mutual defense arrangement. The question then becomes whether the Philippine capability can be upgraded sufficiently (and who would pay the considerable expense involved) so that a genuinely joint air defense plan could be devised. Beyond this are questions of sectoral assignments, sharing of air defense information, and determining who undertakes which defense actions and under what allocation of responsibility.

Questions concerning the military and financial burdens of protecting Philippine air space are part of a much broader issue—the nature and extent of the overall U.S. commitment to the external security of the Philippines. Manila's primary concern has centered around the difference between the key sections of the apparently more binding U.S. obligation under the Atlantic Alliance treaty of 1949 and the MDT obligations of 1951.[78]

Filipinos note that Article V of the NATO treaty "automatically" requires the United States to fight if any of its allies is attacked since it obliges the signatories to assist "by taking forthwith . . . such action as it

---

* Meanwhile, at higher levels, joint U.S.–Philippine training exercises for external security have been sustained, primarily in the air. The Southeast Asian regional cooperative efforts at Crow Valley have also benefited Filipino morale, despite the diplomatic issues of third-country access. In addition to annual bilateral joint exercises, such as the ones at the Philippine base at Fort MacArthur, there are monthly meetings with the U.S. Commander-in-Chief, Pacific (CINCPAC) to discuss logistics, training, operation of the facilities and joint security concerns. Exchanges of intelligence bring the Philippines up to date on Southeast Asian regional developments and the U.S. is briefed on the Philippine internal situation. The Joint Defense Board meets monthly and the Foreign Ministers Council annually.

deems necessary, including use of armed force, to restore and maintain the security of the North Atlantic area." In contrast, Article IV of the MDT states that in case of an armed attack in the Pacific area upon either party, the other will "act to meet the common danger in accordance with its constitutional processes,"[79] a formulation common to other U.S. mutual security pacts. In response to continued Philippine complaints that this treaty in effect lacks binding assurances, U.S. officials, including Secretaries of State John Foster Dulles, in 1954, and Cyrus Vance, in 1979, have stated that the U.S. would regard an attack on the Philippines as a *casus foederis* for implementing the treaty—that is, the U.S. would respond with force.

American specialists do not wish to "clarify" or amend the MDT, holding that it is an unequivocal obligation as it stands[80], but Philippine experts continue to argue that it still falls short of a pledge of guaranteed retaliation because the wording of the treaty remains less clear-cut than in the seemingly more binding NATO statement. In part, Philippine concerns center on the treaty requirement to act through constitutional processes, raising the spectre of congressional delays or even a refusal to honor post-1951 executive branch clarifications of the MDT. Congressional opposition to the Vietnam War in the 1970s and passage of the War Powers Resolution in 1973 intensified these worries, which were not fully assuaged by the Vance assurance that the Resolution did not apply to treaties already in effect at the time of its adoption.[81]

Differences also mark the related issue of the territorial scope of the commitment. The Vance letter of 1979 identified the area of the American commitment as including the "metropolitan territory of the Philippines," defined as including all "land areas and adjacent waters which were ceded to the U.S. by Spain in the Treaty of Paris in 1898 and the Treaty of Washington in 1900."[82] Philippine officials want the pledge to include portions claimed by Manila that lie outside the "metropolitan area" as currently defined[83]—in particular, the Spratley Islands, 250 miles to the west and valued for their strategic location and possible oil and mineral deposits. Beijing, Taipei, and Hanoi have competing claims to the Spratleys; at present the Philippines, Vietnam, Taiwan, and the People's Republic of China each occupy one or more islands. Since the U.S. wishes to avoid involvement in conflicts over disputed zones, it adheres to a strict territorial interpretation of its obligations under the MDT.[84] In a similar vein, the U.S. has resisted Philippine efforts to link the MDT to domestic statutes in which these islands are claimed as part of the nation's territory. There is no likelihood the U.S. will change its position on this issue.

Filipinos also claim some ambiguity about the extent of the American commitment regarding skirmishes in the southern Philippine islands, primarily in the border regions adjacent to Malaysia. In particular, frequent bandit raids and retaliatory incursions in hot pursuit by Malaysian forces are sources of friction. In 1985, for example, a retaliatory Malaysian strike against bandits in a Philippine village led to deaths, abductions, and property damage. The Philippines sought U.S. aid, but the American position was that these low-level activities did not fall under the purview of the MDT.

Another Philippine concern is that both the Communist and Moslem insurgencies could get out of hand and threaten the survival of the state. In the past, inquiries have been made about whether the U.S. would come to Manila's assistance in such a crisis, even though both countries have repeatedly averred that internal security was to be handled by the Philippines. Military cooperation in training and defense planning has therefore been circumspect, in order to avoid giving even the appearance of American support crossing this line of involvement.[85] Thus Manila has hesitated before engaging in joint conventional exercises because it also does not want to create the impression of American involvement in the counterinsurgency war. (Another reason for holding back is the country's lack of resources, even for small-scale exercises).

Management of the Facilities

The American position has been that the amendments to the MBA give the Philippine government a great degree of *control over the facilities,* and that there is little more that could be yielded on this score. The revisions of 1979 and 1983 have been cited as having cleared away all remaining major substantive issues. The Philippines has command over the bases, of which the facilities are a part; at Subic, the U.S. occupies 14,400 acres within the 37,000-acre Philippine base; at Clark there is a 9,000-acre U.S. facility in a Philippine base of 129,000 acres. Philippine sovereignty has been acknowledged and the national flag flies over the bases; criminal jurisdiction is in line with the NATO and Japanese arrangements; CIQ (customs, immigration, and quarantine) arrangements have been adjusted to Manila's satisfaction so that it has the right of inspection in those matters in the U.S. facilities; Philippine officials since 1983 have access to the facility, and a significant portion of land has reverted to the Philippines.

Filipinos acknowledge the importance and validity of many of these changes. Yet, from their perspective many issues remain unsettled, and the concessions obtained have been more symbolic than substantive.[86] We have already noted that Filipinos cite their total lack of control over third-country access to the facilities as evidence that the bases are Philippine in name only. They still see the reversion of sovereignty and the establishment of a Philippine base command as essentially hollow gestures.

The issue here is how to give the Philippines greater control without significantly impairing America's ability to conduct essential operations at Clark and Subic. Authority over the introduction of military units from other Pacific allies is but one case in point.

At the operational level, Clark Field may offer greater opportunities for adjustments than Subic. One issue involves the granting of overflight rights to Philippine Air Lines. This would entail the presence of a Philippine air controller and complicate operations in other ways as well. Though technically feasible, it would require an exception for PAL to the rules of the Chicago Convention, which calls for equal treatment for all commercial carriers. Another change would grant permission to Philippine commercial planes to land at Clark in bad weather as an alternative to Manila International Airport. This raises problems of handling large aircraft on short notice, ramp space, and customs and security considerations. One possibility would be to add an additional, separate runway for commercial air use. But beyond that is the question of joint basing once the Philippine air force regains a modern fixed-wing capability.

For its part, the U.S. may seek changes in arrangements for air training exercises. It may wish to extend the zone allowed for such missions to include mountainous terrain, as well as to expand the range of its activities to improve low-altitude navigation skills. At present the U.S. has to conduct these training exercises elsewhere in the Pacific area.

Change is more difficult to implement at Subic Bay because of the complexities involved in the control of shipping. Key American requirements are to maintain freedom of harbor operations, capacity for maintenance and repair, management of the storage depot, and use of the nearby land-based air strip at Cubi Point. Compromises that do not derogate these functions could blunt potential challenges to continued U.S. use of the facility, but some issues are inherently difficult to resolve. One Philippine aspiration, for example, is to have a greater portion of the area dedicated to profitable commercial activity that would enhance the national economy. Questions of space availability, security of the facility, and unhindered American military use, however, make it difficult for the U.S. to yield much ground.

The U.S. seeks to retain control over Subic Bay and the port, without altering current arrangements under which Philippine vessels require U.S. permission to use these waters. Manila seeks sovereign control over Subic Bay—allowing U.S. movements, but only by permission of the Philippine Subic Bay Commander.[87] As for other commercial endeavors, the presence of a Kawasaki shipyard in the area illustrates the problem. To the U.S. it is an undesirable intrusion. Nor is it profitable for the Japanese, who do not take on sufficient business for fear of becoming involved in work related to U.S. military activities. The U.S. would certainly oppose any effort to allow Soviet ships in Batangas, to the south of the Manila Bay area.

Other modifications to meet Philippine demands involve taxing the gantry crane at Subic or allowing the Philippine armed forces to make purchases from the facility's fuel lines at the lower American price levels. Additional changes at both Clark and Subic could include adjustments in taxation, more purchases from Philippine sources, and greater economic activity at the facilities by Philippine concessionaries.[88]

Philippine officials are also pressing for binding arbitration of labor disputes and seek a revision of the Base Labor Agreement. In 1983 they asked to have Philippine labor law apply to the facilities, and they are bound to raise this issue again.[89] The U.S., however, wishes to retain authority over the selection of workers, for fear that any other arrangement would result in an inefficient labor force.

More substantive responsibilities might be given to the joint bodies assigned to monitor activities at the facilities. There is some disagreement about whether or not they perform useful functions and keep liaison activities on course. The Defense Board meets twice monthly and has recently revised the CIQ procedures, enabling that inspection to flow more smoothly. Similarly, the Criminal Jurisdiction Implementation Committee (CJIC) meets monthly and discusses which party

(U.S. or Philippine) has primary jurisdiction in specific cases, and it resolves these questions with little difficulty, despite sensational Philippine press reports to the contrary. With the recent appointment of new Philippine deputy commanders, coordination at the top level of base/facility management has also proceeded more smoothly than in past years. For example, the deputy base commander handled requests by the Zambeles provincial board for detailed reports on five incidents between 1979 and 1986 in which U.S. jets reportedly dropped bombs accidentally in that province.[90]

Before 1979, the task of providing *base and facility security* fell to the U.S. Marines. Since then, responsibility for the perimeter of the bases and the buffer territory between that line and the facilities themselves has rested with the Philippines. The U.S. handles security within the facilities, with no Philippine police allowed in these enclaves, which are under American authority. Fortunately, this intra-facility arrangement has not become a point of contention because the U.S. would sharply resist any attempt to change it.

A more immediate issue, however, centers on base perimeter security that the Philippine forces have been unable to maintain at an adequate level, leading some American critics to complain that the U.S. yielded too much in the 1979 revisions. The murder of three American servicemen in the Clark-Angeles City area in late October 1987 added to the concern over security arrangements, and joint patrols now cover the entire base and nearby areas as well. Sustained terrorist attacks on Americans in the vicinity of the bases could conceivably raise serious challenges to the effective use of the facilities in the future. Burglaries at the U.S. facilities also continue at a troublesome level and, as joint activities expand, the U.S. may seek greater security authority than it currently has.

Continual scavenger activity in the base area near the American facility line has led to a series of incidents in the recent past in which U.S. security forces and their guard dogs set upon the intruders. These made for spectacular claims of assault in the Philippine press, and accusations of U.S. colonial-rule attitudes. Anti-base nationalists have used these opportunities to the fullest to arouse emotional hostility against the American presence. Philippine lawyers in turn use and expand upon this publicity to strengthen the bargaining position of their clients.[91]

Additional *land reversions* may also be sought by Philippine negotiators, despite the substantial reductions in U.S.-controlled territory made in past revision agreements from the nearly five million acres originally reserved in the 1947 MBA. American defense officials believe that there is little more they can yield at Clark or Subic, though the recreational areas at Camp John Hay and Grande Islande are possibilities. Philippine negotiators have sought Crow Valley in Tarlac and the San Miguel Reservation in Zambeles because of their "valuable and extensive agricultural lands much needed by [the] population...." Crow Valley also provides the only economical route for a road across Luzon,[92] but the U.S. Air Force considers Crow Valley to be a vital training range. This contentious issue will undoubtedly come up again.

In the Subic area, it could be argued that jungle terrain and other territory not essential to the facility's primary function should be turned over to Manila in order to minimize the adverse impact of the anti-base pressure groups in an era of rising Philippine nationalism. But, again, the Americans are reluctant to yield what they consider to be an important training facility.

Beyond these territorial issues are Philippine quests for control over the natural resources on the facilities themselves.[93] The U.S. seeks to retain its power of consent regarding their exploitation, while the Philippine government claims that the power to grant rights of exploitation belongs solely to the territorial sovereign. A similar dispute centers upon U.S. control of the Subic Bay and Clark watersheds and forest areas,[94] which the Philippines seeks to place under Manila's administration. The U.S. fears that despoilation of the forests, as has occurred in other reverted areas, would ruin the ecological balance and critically impair the vital water supply that now sustains these facilities.

Questions of *compensation* for continued American use of these valuable lands frequently come up and will be central to Philippine concerns in the 1988 review and subsequent negotiations.[95] This issue is discussed in detail below. Suffice it to say here that, despite the desire of some Americans to separate payment from the terms of agreement, as a practical matter there is the prospect of a reduction in the amount that the U.S. will be willing to pay should more land revert to Philippine control. Significant downsizing of the facilities and a reduction of activity there would also appreciably lower total direct spending, with significant negative consequences for the Philippine economy. Despite some Philippine claims to the contrary, it is not clear that reversion of lands or the facilities would bring an equivalent benefit to the country, since it is difficult to predict the monetary value of added agricultural activity in an era of uncertain world prices for such products. Even a major reversion of the shipyard facilities at Subic might not bring commensurate benefits, particularly with the world shipbuilding industry in a depressed economic condition.

The general American position on the contentious issue of *criminal jurisdiction* is that, whatever the long history of past Philippine grievances, the issue is now resolved because the guidelines in the NATO and Japanese accords fully apply. The basic Philippine complaint is that before the adoption of the present format, in cases involving Americans and Filipinos the location of the crime was the central fact in determining jurisdiction and the final decision lay with the Philippine Secretary of Justice.[96] Today, the central question is whether the alleged offense committed by American military personnel was in the actual performance of a specific military duty. Under current arrangements, adopted in 1965 and based on the U.S.–Japanese agreement, the U.S. commanding officer issues a certificate of duty. In case of dispute, the matter must be settled by negotiation via diplomatic channels, and therefore the Philippines has lost the power of having its own officials make the final determination. Philippine negotiators have sought to put the matter on a judicial basis by having Philippine courts determine whether official duty was involved or not. Despite their search for NATO parity elsewhere, here they reject such parallel treatment.

Another change sought by the Philippines has been to place an international "hold" on civilian as well as military personnel who are subject to charges under Philippine law. At present, the U.S. guarantees only that military people will not leave the country before completion of their case. For civilians, the U.S. merely guarantees that the accused will not be permitted to depart via military transportation but says it cannot order a civilian to remain. That part is up to the Philippines by checking on departures at Manila International Airport, the commonly used civilian exit route. The Philippines also has sought open access to the American facilities to execute process-serving activities. The U.S. has rejected this in favor of current practice that requires clearance through American military law channels and is implemented by escorting the Philippine official on and off the premises.

The U.S. has complained that it has spent more time and money defending military and civilian personnel in the Philippines than in all the rest of the Pacific Command combined. Many Americans believe this is due to the large number of groundless and specious legal actions brought, especially against civilian personnel. One important category of such cases has arisen from the dismissal of Philippine employees by civilian U.S. officials, who are then sued under the Philippine legal code. (They do not fall under primary U.S. jurisdiction, which presently applies only to those Americans who come under U.S. military law.) The U.S. would like to gain primary jurisdiction over American civilians acting in their official capacity, or failing this, have the MBA modified so as to have the Philippine Secretary of Justice conduct a preliminary review of cases involving official duty actions of U.S. civilian employees in order to expedite the procedure.

Another difficulty confronting the U.S. has been the writs of attachment that may be levied, under the Philippine legal process, against individuals being sued. Since many cases last more than a year, this is a great inconvenience and is often used by plaintiffs as leverage for settling what the U.S. believes to be unwarranted claims. This is particularly onerous in official duty cases. The deliberate pace of the Philippine criminal process, which takes one to one-and-one-half years even in minor traffic cases, makes the commitment to international "hold" of military personnel extremely burdensome. The U.S. would prefer to have a one-year limit on holding American military personnel charged with criminal offenses.

Still more troublesome is the Philippine interpretation of the arrangement under which the U.S. has primary jurisdiction in offenses against the person or property of American military personnel or civilians. The Philippine government holds that this does not apply to cases of chastity and honor, in which Manila claims primary jurisdiction even when both parties are American. The U.S. wants a redefinition and clarification of the arrangement regarding crimes against persons, giving it jurisdiction over all *inter se* criminal cases, that is, those involving only Americans.

The U.S. would also like to adjust the arrangement on compensation for property constructed for U.S. forces in the Philippines. Unlike arrangements in Japan and Korea, the U.S. completely reimburses the Philippines, whereas there is cost-sharing in Korea and Japan bears the total charge. The U.S. would like to share the burden rather than bear fully the charges for the land and all other costs.

Differences over Compensation

One of the severest challenges in renegotiating the American presence at the Philippine facilities lies in the question of compensation. Even the term used to identify the transfer of funds has evolved into a very heated issue, with the U.S. insisting on "compensation," rejecting the Philippine claim that the payment is "rent." The two parties are also somewhat at odds over the relationship between development assistance programs and monies designated as compensation for the bases. Questions of dollar amounts, duration of specific arrangements, specific uses of funds, regularity of incremental deliveries, and the use of aid programs as leverage in other matters make the question of compensation particularly complex and sensitive.

One immediate concern in negotiating new arrangements is the increased pressure in the U.S. to reduce foreign aid. Foreign aid has never been a very popular program in Congress and is likely to suffer further cuts as part of the effort to confront the budget crunch and the national debt. Even appreciation of the strategic importance of the facilities and a desire to sustain the democratic Aquino government may not outweigh congressional concerns over the deficit.[97] At the same time, Philippine officials and political leaders, arguing that their country has been short-changed in the past, are demanding significantly larger sums, commensurate with amounts given to other U.S. allies hosting American forces, particularly Spain, Greece, and Turkey. Even Israel and Egypt, far and away the largest U.S. aid recipients, have been cited by ranking Filipinos as appropriate models for equal treatment.

The demand for greater financial payments is reinforced by the factors noted earlier—alleged derogations of sovereignty, the Philippines' more open and critical domestic political environment, intensified nationalism, and the "nuclear magnet" burden of sustaining the region's security. If compensation levels (or an international mini-Marshall Plan) cannot satisfy Philippine expectations, the two sides might look to other types of economic relations—such as trade preferences or debt relief—in order to devise an acceptable compensatory arrangement. However, each of these alternatives generates its own set of problems and may not readily provide a satisfactory solution.

Current Arrangements. Current compensation arrangements rest on the 1983 revision that promised the U.S. president's "best effort" to obtain $900 million over a five-year period, distributed as follows: $125 million in military assistance grants (MAP), $300 million in foreign military sales (via FMS loans), and $475 million in economic support (including grant budget) funds (ESF). On an annual basis, these totals notionally break down to $180 million a year, with $95 million in economic and $85 million in military assistance. However, the sums were not delivered at this steady rate over the first three years because of congressional hostility to the Marcos regime and its corrupt practices. (As noted, this shift from military to non-military aid was urged by Philippine opposition leaders, many of whom now hold office.) Economic assistance to the country came close to equaling $475 million in the first three years alone, if one combines ESF with regular non-base-related Third World developmental assistance funds. By comparison, military aid comprised $40 million in 1985, $102.4 million in 1986, and $100 million in 1987. (In 1987, half was in supplemental legislation that was eventually approved.) This brought the military total close to the $255 million that might have been anticipated, based on $85 million a year. Furthermore, with several adjustments, repayable FMS loans comprised only $29.4 million of this total, whereas $213.3 million was under non-repayable MAP grants, more than reversing the original proportions, which weighted military (i.e. MAF and FMS) aid toward loans by a margin of more than two to one.[98]

Changes in funding the various categories of assistance and the complex system of congressional appropriation have led some Filipinos to argue that the U.S. has fallen behind in its payments and therefore has failed to fulfill its obligations. In a visit to Manila during June 1987, Secretary of State George Shultz called this accusation unfounded and estimated that U.S. contributions would actually exceed $1 billion by 1989, well above the anticipated original four-year total of $720 million.[99] In this respect, during FY 1985–1987, the U.S. had provided $609.6 million in ESF and $242.7 million in military aid (with MAP comprising $213.3 million and FMS $29.4 million) for a total of $852.3 million as against the notional promise of $540 million ($180 million × 3). For FY 1988, Congress has appropriated $249 million ($125 million MAP and $124 million ESF),[100] as against the "best effort" pledge of $180 million ($85 million military and $95 million ESF) for the year.

Congress has not accepted as binding any multiyear undertakings to provide specific sums of security assistance. "Best effort" pledges have therefore generally been accepted by states that provide use of facilities over extended periods of time. The U.S. view is that a failure to deliver the promised amount in equal annual increments should not jeopardize an agreement that provides for the common defense interests of the two parties. The prevailing sentiment in Washington therefore has opposed viewing these as commercial transactions or contractual arrangements in which the failure of one party to fulfill annual obligations allows the other to terminate the accord. There are, then, sharp differences between the U.S. and the Philippines on all these points—the alleged inadequacy of the "best effort" approach, adherence to agreements on annual sums, and recourse to threats to terminate the accords as a lever for compliance.

Rent. The rent issue stems from the Philippine desire to receive "regular payments" for use of the facilities without any American discretion over annual sums or the yearly makeup of assistance packages.[101] At the time of the initial agreement, President Marcos referred to the payments begun in 1979 as rental fees, but the U.S. Congress continued to decide annually on amounts to be paid and how the funds were to be divided among categories agreed upon. As noted, Philippine insistence on a treaty stipulating fixed sums reflects the determination to receive payment "automatically" and without strings. With a "best effort" undertaking, however, the U.S. can legally withhold assistance without technically violating the agreement and so, it is argued by some Filipinos, exercise a hold over any Philippine government. Theoretically, they believe, Washington could delay payments in order to pressure President Aquino to accede to American demands regarding revisions in the arrangement.[102] Under a rental arrangement, then, Manila would supposedly avoid such pressures and escape the U.S. legislative-executive encounters that often affect the outcome of appropriation bills.

In identifying the payments as rent, the Philippines would be able to claim that the base compensation arrangement should be treated separately from development assistance. Many Philippine officials believe that compensation for the facilities is not aid and should not be presented as such to the American Congress or public. In effect, they argue all economic assistance over $95 million a year (the annual ESF allotment under the "best effort" five-year agreement regarding the facilities) is for development and should not be counted as aid money in return for the facilities. From this perspective, such allocations as the $200 million associated with the Aquino visit of 1986 are independent of the 1983 five-year commitment. Development aid, these officials believe, must be treated on its own merits, not subject to reductions because of the facilities-related ESF appropriations.

Prospects for contractual arrangements, rental or otherwise, run up against strong U.S. resistance. In part, this is a matter of principle and in part it is to avoid setting a precedent in dealing with its southern NATO allies. Secretary of State George Shultz has suggested that, if the bilateral relationship became an essentially commercial deal, it would wither as the U.S. could no longer count on the Philippines as a reliable ally. He said that the U.S. would pull out if the Philippines insists on a purely rental agreement, stating that under such conditions " . . . we don't want to be here."[103] Yet a Philippine legislator stressed the importance of both the American tie and the need for a contractual rental arrangement by noting, "We are not renting it out to whoever wants it. . . . We are not renting this out to the Russians and to the Chinese. . . . We're renting it out to [the Americans]."

Some have wondered whether, despite the significant differences, there is any way the type of commitments made in the Micronesian agreement could be translated into language in agreement with the Philippines going beyond the "best effort" formula.[104] The question is whether this would satisfy Manila and avoid the constitutional and "commercialization" concerns that the rent issue generates for the U.S. Much would, of course, depend on total sums agreed upon and on control over the disbursements. At present, an agreed-upon format for compensation still remains a major issue of contention.

Military Aid. The flow of military aid has emerged as a particularly troublesome issue in recent years. Some argue that the portions withheld in protest against corruption and dictatorial practices during the late Marcos years set an unfortunate precedent in using aid flows as leverage.[105] Others who criticize the U.S. for using aid flow for leverage accepted its validity in this instance—indeed encouraged it at the time.

With the end of the Marcos regime and the attack on the corrupt system that had in effect despoiled the military, as well as other sectors of the society, the armed forces hope to repair the damage and grow at a fairly rapid rate. But, despite assiduous efforts, they still need several more years to make the system efficient. The failure to sustain larger and regular funding of the military at the outset of the Aquino period was especially troublesome, particularly since they came in the wake of cuts in the mid-1980s. These setbacks in the midst of a five-year planning process that centered on spare-parts procurement and modernization, it is argued, gave rise to despair over the utility of such efforts, as unpredictable reductions in the flow of military aid hurt an already weakened armed force and made comprehensive planning impossible. Military officials thus agree with those who have found the "best effort" approach unacceptable, and they too now favor formal American requirements.

They also want much larger sums on more favorable terms, even though the $50 million supplemental for FY 1987 and the $125 million appropriated for FY 1988 would bring the four-year total of military assistance to $367.7 million (as against a nominal "target" of $340 million under the 1983 agreement).[106] The armed forces continue to fault the aid program for its changing totals, uneven flow, limited size, and what they see as its general unpredictability. Philippine military and civilian defense officials are not mollified by the high proportion (90 percent) of grant aid in the total package.* To hard-pressed military leaders, so desperately short of funds, the total amount of resources required over the next four years, rather than grant vs. loan, is the key consideration. Although they prefer direct military aid, in grant form, they support even an increase in economic aid if it leads to greater funding of programs, such as civic actions, that improve the military's image and enhance relations at the local level.

Military leaders point to troop ambushes, defections, and generally low morale that they feel are in large part due to inadequate resource flows. And although the Marcos heritage undoubtedly bears the greatest share of responsibility, and the country's training procedures and maintenance capability have been seriously impaired (and have been responsible for crashes of some newly supplied U.S. helicopters), much of the blame is frequently directed at the U.S.[107] American experts argue, however, that it would take billions of dollars to upgrade the country's inadequate military capability, and that its armed forces' mismanagement has so limited the capacity to absorb assistance effectively that $100 million may be a reasonable annual total over the next few years.[108] This level of help would enable the country to maintain and augment its fleets of helicopters and trucks, selectively buy new equipment, and move supplies to the field more effectively. Critically, this improvement in military assistance is essential to preserve Presi-

* In comparison with other recipients, a larger grant amount is proposed only for Turkey in FY 1988.

dent Aquino's standing with the armed forces and her reputation for being able to receive sustained backing from the U.S.

At the same time, reliability of the aid flow depends not just on the U.S. but also on political developments in Manila. As noted earlier, the U.S. is on record as warning the armed forces, during the August 1987 coup attempt, that a military overthrow of the present government would result in a cutoff of aid, as required by American law.[109] In addition, corruption in the Philippine armed forces is seen as responsible for the draining off of much military aid in the past, and fears of a recurrence are not altogether absent from official U.S. thinking.

Economic Issues. The economic benefit of the bases is a subject of sharp contention. The Philippines holds that it has been cheated all these years and has not derived adequate benefits from its historical relationship with the U.S. This applies to all past transactions, with Marcos in particular accused of striking a bad deal in 1983. The recent annual average of $700 million for Turkey and the five-year $1.12 billion deal with Spain in 1976 have been cited as comparative examples.* (On the other hand, the January 1988 agreement with Spain, in which U.S. air force units were withdrawn from Torrejon air base, ended all further compensation, even though the two sides agreed to extend U.S. use of the other naval and air bases for eight more years.)[110] Philippine officials also note that aid cuts in this period of American austerity have not gone across the board but have exempted the major recipients, particularly the Middle East, from bearing a proportional share of these reductions. That Israel, Egypt, and Pakistan receive these large sums without providing base facilities adds to the sense of unfairness, even though the special circumstances of those countries are well known to Philippine officials and elites.[111]

* For FY 1985 through 1987, U.S. military and economic assistance, in millions of dollars, to five allies was distributed as follows:

	Portugal	**Spain**	**Greece**	**Turkey**	**Philippines**
Total	581.5	1123	1373.5	2225	852.3
of which grants	485.5	355	0	1152	822.9

Thus, whereas three other states received more assistance overall, only Turkey surpassed the Philippines in the all-important grant aid category. Department of State, "Security Assistance to Base Rights Countries," October 1987. See also U.S.I.S., *Background on the Bases*, p.31.

Filipinos also depict the U.S. as a critical and argumentative partner that is always haggling over the terms of assistance, thus reinforcing an image of the U.S. as a selfish power that gives help only to maintain its military presence or to protect that presence against a communist insurgency. Some Filipinos therefore say that they doubt U.S. professions of friendship or concern for their country's well-being.

In Washington, these views are widely seen as reflecting an unfair distortion of the record and grossly underestimating the overall beneficial impact of the facilities. Beyond the $180 million-a-year program related to the facilities, a good deal of the "regular" developmental economic aid program (e.g. $40 million in development assistance in FY 1988 plus $50 million for land redistribution) can be traced to the alliance-facility connection; in terms of its relatively high level of development, the Philippines would normally have received a good deal less than it did. Moreover, Clark and Subic have put a minimum of $1 million a day into the Philippine economy. They employ 45,000 Philippine nationals, and taxes paid by these employees comprise $5.17 million annually.[112] As the second largest employer in the country (after the government itself), the facilities indirectly generate additional income beneficial to economic growth. Secondary sources and their multiplier effect are estimated to run two or three to one and thus to have had a massive positive impact on the economy as a whole.[113] The country's current economic difficulties make the continued presence of the U.S. along roughly current lines practically irreplaceable in the eyes of many observers, including Filipinos.[114]

It is hard to see how additional production of agricultural commodities from reverted base lands could provide income anything like the current levels that the facilities provide. Singapore overcame the massive dislocation caused by Britain's decision to depart (before 1968 Singapore derived about 10 percent of its GNP from British facilities), in part because the port area was readily convertible to use for civilian ship repair and building, at a time of rapid expansion of that industry worldwide. The Philippines would have the capacity to do similar shipyard work today, but it would be in competition with other skilled East Asian rivals, and the shipbuilding and repair market is in a global slump that has already forced some facilities in other East Asian ports to scale down or close. Therefore, even with a smooth transition at Subic, the Philippines could hardly emulate the hard currency incomes and employment achieved a generation ago by Singapore. And there can be no guarantee on the disposition of the dry docks and other equipment if the facilities were closed.

A gap in expectations accompanies these wide differences in estimates of the economic benefits derived from the facilities. Many commentators in Manila have been urging major improvements in U.S. economic concessions, while Americans in Washington have been turning toward a more austere and possibly more protectionist foreign economic posture. Some Filipinos and some American congressional leaders have suggested an international mini-Marshall Plan of up to an additional $1 billion a year.[115] As discussed below, a related proposal calls for special trade access to U.S. markets along the lines of the Caribbean Basin Initiative for a decade or more, but this has been pressed by ASEAN as a whole for some time with little resonance in Washington.[116] The conservative opposition parties also made high levels of assistance part of their campaign platforms in the 1987 legislative election.[117]

Compensation Package. Developing a new compensation package acceptable to both sides will require consideration of many factors. Its size and structure must first of all be related to the duration of the agreement. The terms of any new operational arrangements will be a factor. Timing will also play a role, especially in the relationship between the 1988 review and the negotiation of post-1991 arrangements.

In view of the value of the bases, the fact that the Philippines is a developing country, the relatively modest payments in comparison with other recipients,* and the high cost of arranging alternate facilities, there is little question that both sides anticipate a measurable increase in the level of compensation.

The issues are the sums and conditions acceptable to both parties. The shorter the time period of the arrangement and the fewer the restrictions on the use of the funds, the lower the sum acceptable to the

---

* Sums proposed for FY 88 (with grant portions in parentheses), in millions of dollars, were Portugal 205 (165), Spain 277 (12), Greece 435 (0), Turkey 910 (675), and Philippines 234 (234). Department of State, "Security Assistance to Base Rights Countries," October 1987. Again, only Turkey exceeded the Philippines in the grant category.

Actual appropriations were: Portugal 117, Greece 343, Turkey 547, and the Philippines 249. (With the January 1988 agreement, aid to Spain is to end.) Thus the other three totals declined, while the Philippine total rose; Manila was the only major aid recipient to receive an increase in FY88. *NYT* January 31, 1988.

U.S. is likely to be. Conversely, earmarking and controlling assistance over an extended period would presumably move the total higher. In an intermediate time range, some of the money might be earmarked and some allocated to general budget support.

Because the State Department has had great difficulty in getting its appropriations through Congress, one suggestion has been for the U.S. to place the funds as a line item in the Defense Department budget. Experience demonstrates that the military has less trouble than their diplomatic colleagues in gaining legislative support for costly foreign endeavors. This form of budgeting also might help reduce uncertainties; though the amounts could always be reduced in a given year, the Philippines might regard such an arrangement as evidence of America's good intentions. The stake that the American military has in the facilities also would be made more evident.

U.S. defense officials, on the other hand, almost certainly would prefer to avoid setting such a precedent for negotiations with Greece and Turkey.[118] There is also the Pentagon fear that these allocations would be compensated for by removing other appropriations from the overall defense budget, rather than by having money for the Philippines treated as a special add-on. In that event, American military officials would have to consider difficult trade-offs. While some critics would see such trade-offs as enhancing rationality in defense budgeting, the Pentagon would almost certainly object strenuously.

At this juncture, specifics on compensation and the method of budgeting are, of course, merely conjecture; the key issue is whether the two countries can agree on a framework within which to conduct a good-faith negotiation in order to have reasonable prospects of reaching a satisfactory compromise.

Should the two sides fail to reach agreement based on the amount of the compensation package, there are alternatives: the U.S. could, for example, convert the small amount ($29.4 million) available in FMS credits to grant aid; it could grant special work status privileges for Filipinos in the U.S.; or more broadly, it could extend additional trade benefits, encourage foreign investments, and seek to help the Philippine government alleviate its debt problem. In the area of trade, many Philippine analysts have proposed adopting the formula of the Caribbean Basin Initiative (CBI), which allows products into the U.S. without barriers, or a free trade area, such as have been agreed with Israel and Canada, for an extended period (perhaps equal to the life of a renegotiated facility arrangement). More modest variants have centered upon greater quotas or other beneficial arrangements for such key exports as sugar, textiles, or coconut products.

Each of these issues is very complex, and the specific concessions proposed often run into stiff opposition from U.S. producers,[119] who enjoy significant support in the Congress during this period of U.S. trade deficits and increasing protectionist pressures. The free trade area approach would lead the U.S. to seek reciprocity, which would almost certainly arouse negative Philippine comparisons to the parity requirements under the infamous 1946 Bell Trade Act. As for trade preferences, the Philippines is economically more significant than the Caribbean states, and the list of items excluded from special treatment could become so extensive as to harm the political environment for negotiations. If products such as textiles and shoes were on an exclusion list, the Philippines could even be worse off than it is under the General System of Preferences (GSP) regarding favorable tariffs reserved for Third World countries. (The U.S. has given the Philippines the most generous treatment possible under GSP in recent years.) Thus, further trade concessions may cause significant new problems for both countries; nevertheless, if budgetary considerations keep U.S. money offers at levels unacceptable to Manila, they may be necessary.

Concessions on U.S. investment and debt would be even more difficult, in part because of the more salient and unfettered role of the U.S. private sector in these matters. With regard to direct investment, U.S. multinational corporations (MNCs) had a book value of a modest $3.8 billion in the Philippines in 1986 (about $5.0 billion in replacement value), with additional inflows of only $11.2 million for that year (following a modest $38.0 million for 1985.)[120] U.S. corporations also earned $759 million or 16 percent of the value of all Philippine exports in 1986 and made local purchases of about $360 million that year. Whatever Philippine nationalists may charge about American domination of the economy, U.S. investment has become a great deal less important from the point of view of both countries.

Many analysts believe that a heavy flow of U.S. and Japanese private investment would not only be a great boon to the Philippine private sector but would also help stabilize the political climate and make other potential foreign and domestic investors more confident. Nevertheless, uncertainties over the security situation, over nationalist hostility to

MNCs, and over labor agitation have continued to inhibit a major inflow of American as well as Japanese capital.[121]

In the past year, the Philippine investment climate has improved, and the flow of money into the country has risen. This mild upswing included some repatriated Philippine money as well as some foreign funds. But the improvement has been very gradual, both in adding to existing enterprises and in new investments. The economy did pick up speed through the first half of 1987, helped by the rise in investment and the improvement in world commodity prices, including copra. Factories improved their plant utilization, particularly with regard to consumer durables. Improvements also were notable in the construction industry and in repairing the country's run-down transportation infrastructure. However, the coup attempt of August 28, 1987, and the political aftershocks of that event, reflecting deep instabilities in President Aquino's relationship with the military, had a most disturbing effect. They led to expectations of lower growth in GNP for 1987 than had earlier been projected—of something nearer 5 than 6 percent, still a substantial improvement over past years.[122]

The general point remains that patterns of investment depend on many factors that are often exceedingly difficult to predict. Nor are they subject to direction by any government, least of all by the United States. Investment decisions are subject to many considerations, particularly the growth of the world economy and the alternatives available to any investor. Philippine investment policy is inevitably in competition with that elsewhere, and it is virtually certain that, in such calculations, while the U.S. presence may not attract investors, an American military departure would have a significant negative effect on the inflow of foreign capital. Beyond the signals it would convey about U.S.–Philippine relations in general, assuming aid and investment would be sharply curtailed, the country's ability to contain the insurgency would inevitably arise as a major question. In addition, loss of U.S. military facilities could so impair the Philippine balance of payments that Manila would increase its pressure on foreign firms to hold back on their remittances abroad, an issue that has already been a sore point with foreign investors.

The debt question is even more tangled because the American banks are involved with many other Third World countries whose foreign obligations far exceed the Philippines' $27 billion. Preferential arrangements with one state encourage others to demand similar or even better terms on grace periods, length of loans, rates of interest, or conversions into bonds or other instruments of debt. Numerous banks are engaged in these negotiations—in the Philippine case, twelve on the advisory committee—and many of them have different agendas. The Makati Business Club and some local bankers in Manila have suggested that the U.S. military facilities negotiations be used as leverage to obtain desired rescheduling of payments from bank creditors.[123] There also have been calls in the Philippine cabinet and more recently in the new Philippine legislature for selective repudiation of the debt, adding to the concern of foreign creditors who are simultaneously dealing with a much more massive problem in Latin America. In this situation, the U.S. government can urge major and regional U.S. banks to be as forthcoming as possible, but it cannot impose new arrangements.[124]

Economic benefits more directly related to facility operations might prove more feasible. The two parties could build upon the 1983 agreement to augment the sale of Philippine goods and services to the facilities, engage Philippine construction firms more fully, and expand Philippine utilization of the facilities at reduced charges or on a no-cost basis when possible. Limits to American supplies activities might also be part of this arrangement, although a "Buy Philippine" program that places limitations on American vendors could encounter strong Congressional objections.

Philippine officials have considered Japan and other ASEAN states as possible sources of additional funding for the facilities. Manila looks to Japan because of the latter's wealth, the large sums extended to South Korea, and the onus of war guilt.[125] Many Filipinos believe, with many Americans, that the U.S. military facilities in the Philippines benefit Japan greatly by maintaining that country's vital sea lanes and supporting the global power balance on which Japan's security ultimately depends. In fact, Japan has been increasing its assistance to the Philippines in recent years, with aid now to exceed an annual level of $600 million. It is unlikely to rise significantly above this level in the near future.[126] Because similar security benefits accrue to neighboring states in Southeast Asia, although only Filipinos bear the "nuclear magnet" burden, they are called upon by some Filipinos to contribute to Philippine economic recovery. However, apart from $5 million proffered by Singapore, no such offers have been forthcoming.

Social Problems

The socioeconomic situation in the areas near Clark and Subic, and the towns of Angeles City and Olongapo in particular, loom as a major issue for the Philippines, one that must be dealt with in any renewal arrangement. The U.S. recognizes the costs—of crime, sin, smuggling, and now AIDS in particular—as very real. One feature of the 1983 agreement was an effort to cooperate with Philippine authorities to improve the social and economic conditions in the surrounding areas, much as problems are handled at home or near facilities in other allied lands. To many Filipinos, however, this aid is not enough, or it appears to be poorly applied. To others it is only a sop and the real solution is to close the facilities. Although the bases are strongly supported by local residents, opponents of the American security connection use this emotional issue and the horror stories that periodically capture the headlines to attack the MBA and to seek broader public support for the opposition movement.

Community Relations

Improved community relations comprise an important objective of aid and employment programs aimed at dealing with these social disadvantages. Certainly the developmental assistance and ESF projects involving schools, orphanages, public health, roads, and markets are of some help. The U.S. selects the tasks and then works closely with Philippine officials, including the armed forces, in order to improve their very poor image. In this process, one frustration for Americans is that local political officials frequently claim credit for new infrastructure, like markets, with little notice given to the American contribution.

Americans and Filipinos agree that there is a pressing need for increased funding of local efforts and for related civic action programs by the U.S. military. However, budget cuts and more stringent accounting procedures have reduced programs focused on community relations. This is especially true in comparison with past years when funds, not fully authorized, were used for widespread medical services (emergency medical help is still provided), and surplus equipment could be more easily transferred to the local users. At present, even Americans in the field complain that Philippine access to U.S. equipment is too limited. There is also a general feeling shared by officials of both countries that the facilities themselves are still too sealed off from the nearby areas, even though they have recently been opened to the public and local vendors are now allowed to sell more wares on the premises. But the degree of integration into the wider community and the level of availability of Philippine products remain issues that need further consideration.[127] The Filipinos in Angeles City and Olongapo want to develop new industries and believe that Americans can help. Joint projects (e.g. training programs on how to do business inside the facilities, and skill-development projects in the towns) are also sought.

As an employer, the U.S. has a good reputation for training Filipino workers at the facilities in technically advanced skills, and many of them later find well-paying jobs abroad. The labor force is efficient and loyal, but labor relations are worsening, in part because the wage level, though high by domestic standards, is low in comparison to pay in other countries. This has led to complaints, strikes, and demands for better arrangements in pay and other work-related matters.[128]

An improvement in local economic conditions may help reduce the glaring disparities in living standards around the facilities. Local officials' resentment at the central government for failing to develop the economy and improve social infrastructure (e.g., education) centers on Manila's rationale that these cities already have an "entertainment industry" that generates income and so should not receive substantial funds for new extensive projects.[129]

On a broader canvas, many Filipinos argue that the country must adhere to some form of the MBA in order to get the assistance required to get the economy back on its feet. After that, the country may be able to terminate the arrangement. On the other hand, as the Japanese experience indicates, as the internal economy improves and the local standard of living rises, much of the tension dissipates and the facilities become easier to tolerate. From this perspective, a healthier Philippine economy—or at least the prospect of one—might afford a firmer foundation for a renewed MBA and give the American military presence the political durability that it seeks. The history of such facilities indicates that their social impact will continue to generate tensions and requires close attention throughout the renegotiation period and beyond, should the facilities remain.

ASEAN and Japan

The ASEAN Position: Non-Involvement but Concern. The ASEAN organization composed of six Southeast Asian nations may appear somewhat tenuous and limited, but it has held together under difficult circumstances for almost two decades. It has acted as a group in dealing with the developed world on issues of international trade and in opposing the Hanoi-dominated regime in Cambodia. Though purporting not to be a security organization, it has opposed Vietnam's occupation of Thai border areas and is generally concerned about regional security and stability as well as economic policies on investment and trade.[130] It seeks to avoid the collapse of any member state for fear of its destabilizing effect on the whole region. And while it moves slowly in building consensus and tries to avoid contentious issues, ASEAN has proven resilient. Through its ministerial-level meetings it has fostered the development of a web of personal relations that have grown in strength and importance over the years.

The tradition of cautious and limited cooperation is reflected in ASEAN's care not to infringe on the sovereignty of its members or to interfere in matters considered sensitive by the individual states. A commitment to nonalignment and eventual neutrality—as expressed in the 1971 ZOPFAN declaration sponsored by Malaysia and reaffirmed at the ASEAN summit in Manila in December 1987—reinforces the nonsecurity orientation of the association and further complicates ASEAN's relationship to the Philippine base issue. To reinvigorate this commitment to neutrality, in 1987 Indonesia, supported by Malaysia, sponsored a Southeast Asian Nuclear Weapons Free Zone (SEANWFZ).[131]

In reality, there is very strong sentiment in Thailand, Singapore, and Brunei, and among some Indonesian and Malaysian officials, for a continued American presence in the Philippines. The reasons are: to balance a perceived rise in Soviet power, anticipation of increased Chinese and Japanese influence in the area, a desire to keep an unstable Philippine regime on its feet, and the realization that regional stability is essential if the area is to attract continued U.S., Japanese, and European trade and investment.

Sea lane protection, greater likelihood of aid in an emergency, and a deterrent influence on Vietnam are further perceived benefits of a continued U.S. presence. If the U.S. were to leave the Philippines, ASEAN might suffer internal division between those concerned about Moscow and those concerned about Beijing, thus endangering the record of cooperation achieved in the past fifteen years.

Some ASEAN members place special emphasis on the value of the U.S. presence as a counterweight to the Soviets in Vietnam.[132] As noted, one can turn this argument around to justify the Soviet presence as balancing the U.S., with the departure of both treated as an even trade-off. In fact, however, even if Soviet access to Cam Ranh Bay ended, the United States would consider its own global interests importantly served by continued access to Clark and Subic, which relate to security concerns well beyond the region of Southeast Asia.

The Issue of ASEAN Support. ASEAN's non-aligned tradition, the need to operate by consensus, and its lack of responsibility for security matters make it most unlikely that the organization itself will voluntarily support continuation of the U.S.–Philippine arrangement. Malaysia and Indonesia in particular, as sponsors of ZOPFAN and SEANWFZ, are committed to the doctrine of neutrality and do not wish to impair their standing in the non-aligned world.[133] Moreover, a statement of support would move the organization into uncharted and possibly dangerous waters, since it would not be clear what obligations the member nations would incur. Thus, Foreign Secretary Manglapus could not generate discussion of the bases at the ASEAN summit.[134]

On the other hand, ASEAN's caution and the recognition of strategic realities caused SEANWFZ to be adopted only "in principle" as a goal for ASEAN to pursue, but not as a near-term objective.[135] Many present ASEAN leaders agree that a continued U.S. presence in the Philippines is desirable, an orientation that contributed to their careful treatment of the nuclear-free-zone concept.[136] Still, SEANWFZ will be cited by Philippine opponents of the facilities in the coming debates.

There is no security structure similar to NATO, a lack some observers perceive as part of a strategic-political vacuum in East Asia that the ASEAN states are not prepared to fill, even in part, by getting together to help the Philippines through making and maintaining a commitment. In addition, while the ASEAN states see an economic role for Tokyo, they generally oppose any Japanese security responsibility for sea lanes beyond the current limit of 1,000 miles from Tokyo.[137]

Japan: Value of the Philippine Facilities. The Japanese view their security as importantly linked to a continued U.S. military presence in the Philippines. As integral parts of the vital U.S. military structure in East Asia, Clark and Subic appear important to maintain the credibility of U.S. power and to deter Soviet meddling and pressure tactics in the region. The U.S. position in the Philippines sustains three major interrelated Japanese interests: open sea lines of communication (SLOCs), the presence of the 7th Fleet, and the overall stability and security of the region.

In undertaking its SLOC responsibility to the south, Japan is counting on a robust U.S. effort to sustain this vital lifeline in the area beyond the 1,000 mile range. The 7th Fleet is a unified force that relies on both Japanese and Philippine facilities in an integrated manner. Although they have different functions, the Japanese consider Subic and Yokosuka as one strategic unit, and hold the same view about the air bases at Clark and Kadena.[138] Tokyo notes that its 1960 Mutual Security Treaty (MST) with the U.S. aims at the peace and stability of the Far East and not just the defense of Japan. The facilities in Japan may also be used for the protection of the Philippines, which is within the MST's perimeter, as well as to counter threats to the region arising from outside the Far Eastern theater.[139] It is within this security framework that Japanese officials expect the Philippine facilities to work in conjunction with those in Japan to enhance the peace and stability of the Far East. In Tokyo's eyes, limiting U.S. facilities to Northeast Asia west of Guam would have a distinctly negative effect on Japan's security.[140]

Although Japan does not expect to enter a war with the Soviet Union, it is concerned about coping with increased Soviet military activity in East Asia. Moscow's improved access to North Korea (including overflights enroute between Cam Ranh and Vladivostok) and Soviet naval exercises in the Yellow Sea are cases in point. Japan perceives the Soviets as ultimately seeking to dominate the Sea of Japan and become a significant power in the East China Sea—to turn these assets into diplomatic value, and, as the dominant power in the region, to gain the upper hand in bargaining with other states. The Japanese government expects an increase in Soviet–Vietnamese–North Korean military cooperation and sees the U.S. position in the Philippines as a vital counterbalance to Soviet aspirations.

In a still broader perspective, Japanese officials see the U.S. role in the Philippines as serving a global as well as regional security function. Many Japanese are especially concerned about SEANWFZ, which they regard as a troublesome and potentially harmful complication of present arrangements. If ASEAN adopted a nuclear-free zone that allowed each member state to decide how to apply it, this conceivably could prove acceptable to Tokyo, provided the Philippines did not adopt a strict interpretation forbidding visits by naval vessels. Doubtless, Japanese officials prefer that all American allies have a consistent and similar policy on U.S. ship movements rather than risk having antinuclear movements in other lands rekindle anti-base sentiments in Japan. They are worried that the Philippines may not grasp the significance of this matter and hope to preserve the NCND policy through quiet diplomacy with the ASEAN states.

If the U.S. Withdraws. An American withdrawal from the Philippines could come as a serious blow to U.S. credibility in Japan and throughout the Asia–Pacific region. The Japanese recall the consideration of this possibility near the end of the Marcos era, and hope that, if a withdrawal were unavoidable, proper preparations, an orderly departure, evidence of good faith efforts to stay, and the development of effective alternative arrangements to provide continued U.S. naval and air presence in the region would contribute to making such departure more manageable. One concern would be the likelihood of U.S. requests for additional facilities in Japan. But they would find that easier to accommodate than an eventual drawdown of American military strength from Japan, precipitated by a resurgent unilateralist American mentality in the wake of ouster from the Philippines.

Japan's two most urgent concerns about a U.S. withdrawal from the Philippines would center on the situation in Korea and on increased Soviet military activities in the area. While one should not exaggerate the likely impact on Japan, particularly if the United States acted to compensate for this departure with other types of deployment, one would need to be attentive to its effect, in combination with other developments, on Japanese perceptions of the U.S. role in Asia. The Japanese would also be concerned that, following a U.S. departure from the Philippines, Thailand would conclude that the United States could no longer be relied on and would move strategically closer to China, thus causing considerable tension within ASEAN.

Meanwhile the two allies would have to deal with specific aspects of a negative outcome in the Philippines. The first question centers on security of the SLOCs. Since the Japanese and U.S. efforts now supplement each other, a loss of the American facilities would leave the Japanese to worry about protection of this lifeline beyond 1,000 miles from Tokyo. Japan could become so intimidated by an expanded Soviet threat that it would limit its patrol activities even within the 1,000 mile zone. Thus, paradoxically, U.S. withdrawal from the Philippines could increase American responsibilities for patrolling in Northeast Asia. A relocated American presence in the area might also entail more U.S. forces in Japan, with the west Kyushu port of Sasebo a likely candidate, given the physical and political constraints in Okinawa.

On the other hand, the Japanese reaction to the loss of U.S. facilities in the Philippines could be a further buildup of Japanese power, for example to cover 1,500 miles of SLOC.[141] Since antisubmarine warfare (ASW) capability is the most urgent need and submarines provide the best ASW weapons, construction of Japanese submarines could well proceed. Although embedding such a buildup in the U.S.–Japan security relationship and careful prior discussions with other states could limit the damage, an increase in Japanese power and responsibilities would cause great concern in the region. The Chinese response would undoubtedly be hostile. If the Chinese augmented their naval buildup in turn, it could cause considerable unease in Southeast Asia as well.

Even without such a Chinese reaction, the ASEAN states would be very concerned over a Japanese naval buildup and expanded SLOC zones. Just the present 1,000 mile arrangement aroused anxiety and required careful explanations before the Philippines and others gave their wary acceptance. The idea of an increased Japanese role beyond 1,000 miles to compensate for a reduced U.S. presence would be difficult to live with.

Finally, Seoul would be very concerned about Tokyo's increased military capability and role in East Asia, though this might be mitigated by an increased U.S. presence in Japan, particularly if the U.S.–Japan alliance remained firm. However, the Koreans—like the Japanese, the Chinese, and many Southeast Asians—would be seriously concerned by the implications for their own security of a U.S. departure from the Philippines, whatever compensatory moves were undertaken by Japan or the United States.

Japanese Support in U.S.–Philippine Negotiations. The Japanese may quietly explain to the Philippine government their perception of the importance of the facilities in the current world situation. Tokyo is also well aware of the significance of economic assistance to help stabilize the Philippines and to bolster the Aquino regime, as well as to improve the prospects of U.S.–Philippine base negotiations. At the highest level, the Japanese have said that they would do their best to strengthen the Philippine economy and so broaden the joint U.S.–Japanese effort to support that country.

However, there are some serious problems facing both the diplomatic and economic approaches. The history of Philippine antagonism toward Japan and recurrent surges of anti-Japanese sentiment hamper Tokyo's ability to advocate its own perception of the security problem, though exchanges among academic security experts can help. Equally important is a widespread view in Japan that the current Philippine administration is weak and that the government is operating under near-chaotic conditions. The Japanese government continues to support the Aquino regime, but the business community is unhappy with the political-economic environment in Manila and has a hesitant attitude toward investment. There also persists concern in Tokyo that Philippine corruption is siphoning off much of the aid from abroad.

Still the Japanese intend to continue their aid program to the Philippines, which at $600 million a year makes Manila the largest recipient of Tokyo's loan/grant package. With a new aid program and visits by high-level business groups, Japan gives every indication of staying on this course, a policy reinforced by its December 1987 commitment of a $2 billion aid/investment package for ASEAN as a whole.[142]

Although the Japanese would be upset if pressed to link assistance publicly to the retention of the U.S. facilities, a desire to help sustain a strong U.S. military presence in the Philippines is an important motivating factor. Some Japanese would, thus, want to reduce aid if the facilities were gone. Working against deep cuts in its aid program if the U.S. forces departed, however, would be Japan's wish to sustain the existing government, uphold its own image as a generous partner, and more generally strengthen its economic links with ASEAN. The need for regional stability would be greater than ever under these circumstances and, especially if Japan is to play a larger military role in the area, it would want to stay on good terms with its neighbors, who view it with a degree of suspicion. Above all, it would not wish to be treated as a U.S. accomplice under the difficult circumstances that would result from an end to the American–Philippine facility arrangement and a general decline in relations between Washington and Manila.

Fred Greene earned his Ph.D in international relations from Yale University. He is currently A. Barton Hepburn Professor of Political Science at Williams College. He was Director of the Office of East Asian and Pacific Research in the Bureau of Intelligence and Research, Department of State, and a consultant to the National Security Council. He is the author of many books and articles on U.S. policy in Asia.

Notes

1. William E. Berry, Jr. *American Military Bases in the Philippines,* unpublished Ph. D. dissertation (Ithaca, NY: Cornell University, 1981). A short version of Berry's history is included on p. 130. An updated version of the MBA, consolidating all past amendments, can be found in "The 1947 Military Bases Agreement, As Amended", *Foreign Relations Journal,* Vol. 1, no. 3, Manila, September 1986, pp. 169–192. This is based on a compilation, Pacifico A. Castro, ed., *Agreements on U.S. Military Facilities in Philippine Military Bases.*
2. All six facilities are located on Luzon. The rest site is at Camp John Hay in Baguio City. The three smaller installations are a joint air-defense radar complex at Wallace Air Station in La Union, the San Miguel Naval Communication Station in Zambeles, and Camp O'Donnell, a transmitter site with installations in Capas, Tarlac. See U.S. Information Service, *Background on the Bases,* 1986, pp. 5–14.
3. These and other complexities are discussed in Evelyn Colbert, *The United States and the Philippine Bases* (Washington, D.C., The Johns Hopkins Foreign Policy Institute, 1987), pp. 1–2, 14–19.
4. Robert Pringle, *Indonesia and the Philippines: American Interests in Island Southeast Asia* (New York: Columbia University Press, 1980), p.61. See also *The Philippines: Facing the Future,* a report by The Asia Society (New York, 1986), p.29.
5. Alva Bowen discusses various possibilities and the factors affecting them in his paper on p. 105 of this volume.
6. Foreign Secretary Raul Manglapus has expressed the sentiment in terms of a need to end "the American father image." *New York Times (NYT)* December 28, 1987.
7. See Foreign Broadcast Information Service, Daily Report, East Asia (hereinafter FBIS), "Senior DFA Official Urges Closure of U.S. Bases," March 9, 1987.
8. Jacob W. Ulvila and Mark McDonough, "United States–Philippines Military Base Negotiations," prepared as a case study (Cambridge, Massachusetts: Harvard College, 1978), p.9.
9. FBIS, March 9, 1987.
10. FBIS, Narciso G. Reyes, "Base Agreement's Effect on Independence Viewed," June 18, 1986.
11. See for example Narciso G. Reyes, "Scenario on the Bases Issue," *Foreign Relations Journal,* Vol. 1, no. 3, September 1986, pp. 81–94.
12. FBIS, "Anti-U.S. Sentiment Said Growing in Military," October 30, 1987.
13. Jose W. Diokno, "Statement on the 1983 Memorandum of Agreement on the Military Bases," *Foreign Relations Journal,* Vol.1, no.1, January 1986, p. 185.

14. FBIS, "Anti-U.S. Sentiment Said Growing in Military," October 30, 1987.
15. *NYT* September 5 and 7, 1987. For a retrospective analysis, see *NYT* October 1, 1987. On Admiral Hays' role, see *NYT* October 25, 1987.
16. See the speech by David SyCip, "The Bases Question," given at the National Defense College of the Philippines, September 4, 1987.
17. Ambassador Reyes called this American operational autonomy incompatible with national sovereignty, and "places into question the authenticity of Philippine independence." FBIS, June 18, 1986.
18. Colbert, *op. cit.*, p. 2.
19. Recent statistics reflect the modest level of direct U.S. investment in the Philippines which, at $1.1 billion, is half the amount invested in Singapore, one-third of the total in Hong Kong, and one-quarter of the amount in Indonesia. U.S. Department of Commerce, *Survey of Current Business*, Vol. 67, no. 6, June 1987, p. 43.
20. Such was the position espoused by Ambassador Emmanuel Pelaez, "The Military Bases in the Philippines: The Past and the Future," *Foreign Relations Journal*, Vol. 1, no.1, January 1986, pp. 31–34.
21. Senate President Jovito Salonga has stressed Philippine dependence on the U.S. and its lack of a truly independent foreign policy, implying that this is due in good part to the American military presence. FBIS, "Salonga Tests Conditions for Closing Bases," November 9, 1987.
22. FBIS, "Poll Shows Manilans Favor Retaining Bases," June 23, 1986.
23. See testimony of Major General James C. Pfautz (Retired) and Admiral S.R. Foley (Retired) in "Assessing America's Options in the Philippines," Committee Print, submitted to the House Committee on Foreign Affairs, 99th Congress, 2d. session, February 3, 1986, pp. 97–98.
24. Report on the Philippine Social Science Council National Opinion Survey of September 1985, p. 32. Yet the Public Opinion Report published in Manila by the Ateneo-Weather Statistics in June 1986 found that of those aware of the American presence, 50 percent agreed that the U.S. military facilities should stay in the Philippines in comparison with 19 percent who disagreed and 26 percent who were undecided.
25. For example, see FBIS, "Anti-American Neurosis Noted," October 13, 1987, and *NYT* September 5, 1987.
26. Ambassador Reyes, FBIS, June 18, 1986.
27. Colbert, *op. cit.*, p. 18. The Philippines did succeed in getting interest rates lowered by both commercial creditors and international organizations, and in improving the terms of repayment by the end of 1987. See *NYT* December 26, 1987.
28. Colbert, *op. cit.*, p. 18.
29. Since the constitution requires approval by two-thirds of the 24-member Senate for a treaty, it would normally take nine votes to block it. However, since Senator Raul Manglapus became foreign secretary in October 1987, it may require only eight negative votes to block a two-thirds

majority in a 23-member body. Early Philippine senatorial efforts to deal with the base question are reflected in FBIS, "Senators Comment after Touring U.S. Base," September 1, 1987, and "Subcommittee Starts Study of U.S. Bases," September 4, 1987. See also James Clad, "The Bases Are Loaded," *Far Eastern Economic Review,* August 6, 1987, pp. 10–17.

30. Note the shift in attitudes during March 1987 as reflected in FBIS, "Aquino Candidates Said to Oppose U.S. Bases," March 10, 1987, and "Aquino Candidates to Honor U.S. Bases Agreement," March 20, 1987.
31. Berry, *op. cit.,* chapter 5.
32. Ambassador Reyes posits a possible five-year extension with the option to terminate on one year's notice in "Scenario on the Bases Issue," *op. cit.,* 92.
33. See, for example FBIS, "Laurel on Changes in Perceptions of Bases," in which Vice President Salvador Laurel stated, "All bases must go sooner or later. When they have to go is a matter that will be dictated by the national interest." September 10, 1987.
34. The Constitutional Commission of 1986 formally adopted the constitution on October 15, 1986.
35. This is not to say that there was no strong opposition to the new arrangement. One example of this is Pablo Tangco, "The Self-Destructive Philippine Constitution of 1986," Manila 1986 (privately printed).
36. Some Filipinos defend the provision by asserting that the Philippine constitution does not dictate that the U.S. do anything, but mandates only what the Philippine government must do.
37. For a recent version of the annual struggle over congressional funding for the U.N. and related functional organizations, see *NYT* November 24, 1987.
38. Portugal made such threats in 1987 and the issue is still to be resolved. *NYT* September 9, 1987.
39. More generally, as Flora Lewis has observed, "The difference between the major and minor European alliance members is that the first see U.S. efforts as the bulwark of their own defense, and some of the second are tempted to use bases as hostages for their other demands." "Bases as Hostages," *NYT* September 15, 1987.
40. See *U.S. v. Belmont,* 301 U.S. 324 (1937) and *U.S. v. Pink,* 315 U.S. 203 (1942).
41. *NYT* October 4, 1987 reported U.S. concern that acceptance of sweeping restrictions on the American military presence in Spain would lead others, including the Philippines, to follow suit.
42. "U.S. Military Installations in NATO's Southern Region," Report prepared for the Subcommittee on Europe and the Middle East, House Committee on Foreign Affairs, 99th Congress, 2d session, October 7, 1986, pp. 10–11.
43. Bishop Bacani and Commissioner Christian S. Monsod at a November 19, 1986 meeting in Manila sponsored by the Bishops–Businessmen's Council for Human Development.

44. FBIS, "Reagan Effigy Burned in Rally Outside Air Base," February 17, 1987. Senator Wigberto Tanada referred to a U.S. naval visit to Subic Bay as a violation of the constitutional anti-nuclear provision. FBIS, August 27, 1987.
45. FBIS, "Enrile on Constitution, Nuclear Arms, U.S. Base," April 7, 1987.
46. *NYT* August 23, 1987.
47. See a restatement by Enrile of his position in favor of more explicit flexibility after being elected senator, FBIS, "Probe on Nuclear Weapons at Base Urged," August 27, 1987. See also Vice President Laurel's observation that "The presence of superpower forces inevitably involves at the very least the possibility of the introduction, if not the storage or deployment, of nuclear weapons." FBIS, "Laurel on Changes in Perception of Bases," September 10, 1987.
48. See the exchange in 1975 between Paul Barringer and Eduardo Z. Romualdez, in Romualdez *A Question of Sovereignty* (Manila, 1980), p. 108.
49. William Arkin and Richard Fieldhouse, *Nuclear Battlefields* (Cambridge, MA: Ballinger Publishing House, 1985), survey the question of storage on p. 228. F. A. Mediansky, "The U.S. Military Facilities in the Philippines," *Contemporary Southeast Asia*, Vol. 8, no.4, Canberra, March 1987, cites this study and also considers this issue on p. 313.
50. Acting Foreign Minister Pacifico A. Castro, "An Official Interpretation," *Foreign Relations Journal*, Vol. 1, no. 1, January 1986, pp. 186–187, in response to Diokno, *loc. cit.*, pp. 183–184.
51. David SyCip, "U.S. Bases in the Philippines and Philippine Economic Recovery Measures," Manila 1986, p.1. (hereinafter SyCip *loc. cit.*)
52. These are listed in Romualdez, *op. cit.*, p. 279, and discussed in detail, pp. 280–297. This was also raised by one senior Philippine official in May 1987, but another observed in October that Manila might not adhere so strictly to this decade-old position. Author's interviews.
53. Pelaez, *loc. cit.*, p. 27.
54. Narciso G. Reyes, "The Case of the Captive Country," *Foreign Relations Journal*, Vol. 1, no.1, January 1986, a review of the Romualdez book, p. 225. The Reyes piece in FBIS, June 18, 1986, cites the 1976 Philippine draft calling for express consent of the Philippines on use of the facilities for foreign military combat operation. Text of the 1976 draft is in Romualdez, p. 440.
55. *NYT* August 23, 1987.
56. Romualdez, *op. cit.*, pp. 204-205 and p. 441.
57. *Ibid*, p. 441.
58. See Diokno, *loc. cit.*, p. 183 and Romualdez, *op. cit.*, p. 441.
59. For the text of the 1983 revision, see *Foreign Relations Journal*, Vol. 1, no. 1, January 1986, pp. 200–205. It is also in TIAS no. 10699, June 1, 1983.
60. Ramash Thakur, *In Defense of New Zealand: Foreign Policy Choices in the Nuclear Age* (Boulder, CO: Westview Press, 1986). For a more optimistic,

though cautionary, view of New Zealand's impasse with the U.S., see Steve Hoadley, *New Zealand's Defense Policy and the ANZUS Dispute* (Singapore: Singapore Institute of International Affairs, 1986).
61. SyCip, *loc. cit.* argues that on this basis ASEAN should contribute to the economic rehabilitation of the Philippines.
62. See statements by Senator and then Foreign Secretary Raul Manglapus, FBIS, "Philippine Senator on Rebels, U.S. Bases," October 7, 1987; "Manglapus Interviewed on Foreign Policy," October 21, 1987; "Manglapus Interviewed on Bases, ASEAN," November 24, 1987.
63. FBIS, "Enrile on Constitution, Nuclear Arms, U.S. Bases," April 7, 1987.
64. FBIS, "Aquino Opens Summit," December 14, 1987. After emphasizing her observations on the role played by the facilities in enhancing the security of the region, press coverage in Manila went on to call for others to help pay for the bases. FBIS, "Aquino Gives 'Broad Hints' on U.S. Bases," December 17, 1987. According to some accounts, President Aquino's remarks surprised—and dismayed—other officials, including in the foreign ministry, who later tried to explain away what she said as merely reporting the views of others.
65. Narciso G. Reyes, FBIS, June 18, 1986.
66. For a journalistic view of this issue, see Teodoro M. Locsin, "To Hell with the U.S. Bases?," *Philippine Free Press,* September 6, 1986. For a scholarly article that, however, concentrates on a Soviet nuclear assault against the Philippines in isolation, see Serafin D. Talisayon, "Consequences of Nuclear Attack on the Military Bases," *Foreign Relations Journal,* Vol. 1, no. 2, June, 1986, pp. 89–114.
67. FBIS, "Senior DFA Official Urges Closure of U.S. Bases," March 8, 1987.
68. SyCip, *loc. cit.,* notes that in a nuclear war other targets would have higher priority than those in the Philippines and that the effect of such a war would be very harmful to the Philippines in any event.
69. On the other hand, the need to be supportive of U.S. arms control efforts by not disturbing the strategic balance at a critical juncture has been noted by Pelaez, *loc. cit.,* p. 27.
70. *Economist,* August 16–22, 1986, pp. 22–23.
71. Geoffrey Kemp, "U.S. Military Power in the Pacific: Problems and Prospects; Part I," *Adelphi Papers* no. 216. (London: Institute for Strategic Studies, 1987), pp. 47–50.
72. This discussion draws upon Alva M. Bowen, Jr., "The Philippine–American Defense Partnership," in *Rebuilding A Nation: Philippine Challenge and American Defense Policy,* Carl H. Lande ed. (Washington, DC: Washington Institute Press, 1987).
73. A map on p. 120 of Alva Bowen's paper in this volume shows the radius of Soviet air power projection from Cam Ranh Bay, graphically illustrating the increased Soviet presence in the area.

74. Purificacion V. Quisumbing, "ASEAN and China," *Foreign Relations Journal,* Vol. 1, no. 1, January 1986, pp. 149–150.
75. Even this effort depends on extensive U.S. funding. The then Defense Secretary, Raphael Ileto, estimated that the nation's defense budget would have to be doubled if it were to stand on its own in security matters. FBIS, "Ileto Says U.S. Prepares Base Initiative," September 1, 1987.
76. Among the many evaluations of the army's difficult position today are Carolina G. Hernandez, "Security Issues and Policies: The Philippines in the Mid-1980's," *Foreign Relations Journal,* Vol. 1, no. 1, January 1986, pp. 64–81, and The Asia Society, *op. cit.,* pp. 23–26.
77. Colbert, *op. cit.,* p. 16.
78. Romualdez, *op. cit.,* chapter 18, especially pp. 258–260.
79. TIAS 2529.
80. Ambassador Pelaez holds a similar view, *loc. cit.,* p.25.
81. Berry, *op. cit.,* p. 373.
82. TIAS 9224.
83. Pelaez, *loc. cit.,* p. 28.
84. Colbert, *op. cit.,* p. 16 and Pelaez, *loc. cit.,* p. 28.
85. While acknowledging difficulties in conducting the counterinsurgency effort, Defense Secretary Ileto took pains to rule out the participation of foreign troops. FBIS, "Ileto Rules Out Use of Foreign Troops in Fighting NPA," March 7, 1987.
86. SyCip, *loc. cit.*
87. Romualdez, *op. cit.,* p. 282.
88. Some of these measure were adopted in the fall of 1987. *NYT* October 25, 1987.
89. The Labor Secretary seeks to have this resolved prior to any new base agreement. FBIS, "Labor Terms Precondition for Base Talks," December 2, 1987.
90. FBIS, "U.S. Bombing Issue Included in Base Review," March 16, 1987.
91. See for example FBIS, "Lawyer Says U.S. Guards Assaulted Youths," March 19, 1987.
92. Romualdez, *op. cit.,* p. 281.
93. Ambassador Reyes pressed for full control over the natural resources in question, FBIS, June 18, 1986.
94. Romualdez, *op. cit.,* pp. 280, 283.
95. David SyCip made an extensive calculation based on the size of the U.S. facilities in estimating a "straight annual base fee." *loc. cit.*
96. Romualdez, *op. cit.,* pp. 290–291.
97. Colbert, *op. cit.,* p. 19.
98. Figures are calculated from Department of State release, "U.S. Security Assistance to the Philippines," October, 1987.
99. FBIS, "Legislators Assess Shultz Remarks on Bases," June 18, 1987.
100. Department of State, "Philippine MBA 'Best Effort' Pledge vs. U.S. Security Assistance to the Philippines," October 20, 1987; in addition, the

FY1988 appropriations contained $40 million in development aid and $50 million for land redistribution programs, bringing the year's overall total to $349 million. *NYT* January 11, 1988.
101. SyCip, *loc. cit.*
102. Diokno, *loc. cit.*, p. 184. Also, FBIS, "Foreign Office Official Views Problems in Base Pact," July 24, 1987.
103. FBIS, "Legislators Assess Shultz Remarks on Bases," June 18, 1987.
104. Colbert, *op. cit.*, p. 19. Though the Micronesian agreement to provide $2 billion over 50 years was backed by the "full faith and credit of the United States"—a more formal commitment on compensation than the "best effort" pledge—this must be seen against a background of the recipients' acceptance of a long-term provision for American military access and denial of such access to others.
105. Diokno, *loc. cit.*, p. 184.
106. Department of State, "U.S. Security Assistance to the Philippines," October 1987; *NYT* January 11, 1988.
107. Although Philippine military officials acknowledge these accidents were due to inadequate maintenance or poor flying, some Filipinos have charged they were due to the allegedly low quality of the planes, a criticism that the Americans reject. Half of the fifty-four UH-1H helicopters were grounded in mid-1987. *NYT* September 15, 1987.
108. Both sides of the argument on the country's capacity to absorb aid are presented in *NYT* October 25, 1987 and January 11, 1988.
109. Philippine military personnel are reported to have suspected the U.S. of involvement in the August coup effort. FBIS, "Anti-U.S. Sentiment Said Growing in Military," October 30, 1987. Richard Kessler argues that many Filipinos are making a grave error in focusing on alleged right-wing American support of coup plots, when they should be facing the real problems of reform in their country. *NYT* November 6, 1987.
110. *NYT* January 15, 1988.
111. FBIS, "Foreign Department Recommends Higher Base Rentals," June 12, 1987.
112. FBIS, "Aquino Candidates to Honor U.S. Bases Agreement," March 20, 1987.
113. These arguments are developed in U.S.I.S., *Background on the Bases*, pp. 16–22.
114. On the importance of the Subic facility to Olongapo, see "Olongapo City Dead Unless Vessel Docks," *Manila Bulletin*, November 17, 1987.
115. Interview with senior Philippine official, October 30, 1987; Richard Kessler, *U.S. Policy Toward the Philippines after Marcos*, Policy Paper 37 (Muscatine, IA: Stanley Foundation, 1986) p. 18. See also *NYT* November 29, 1987 for "Marshall Plan" type international support of $1 billion a year for five years advocated by Representatives Jack Kemp and Stephen Solarz, along with Senators Alan Cranston and Richard Lugar.

116. See in particular David SyCip, "A CBI Arrangement to Help Philippine Economic Recovery that Should Benefit the U.S. as Well," 1986 (privately printed).
117. FBIS, "Opposition Stance Reported," March 20, 1987.
118. More generally, the interlocking nature of the base system and of the problems in dealing with host countries leads the U.S. to fear that significant concessions or restrictions of any kind in one country will lead others to try to follow suit. This problem, in reference to the Mediterranean allies and the Philippines, has gained greater attention in recent months. See *NYT* October 4, 1987; *Washington Post,* November 24, 1987; and *Wall Street Journal,* December 29, 1987.
119. The U.S. policy of reducing quotas for sugar imports, thus keeping domestic prices high and so not subsidizing domestic producers with direct funding, has brought the 1988 total of sugar imports down by 75 percent from its 1982 level. It now stands at 750,000 tons and may approach zero in a few years. The U.S. has made an exception for the Philippines and the Caribbean states for 1988, allowing 400,000 additional tons to be imported (of which 140,000 tons are allocated to the Philippines), but only if the refined product is re-exported. *NYT* December 16 and 21, 1987 and January 1, 1988.
120. American Chamber of Commerce of the Philippines, "U.S.–MNC Corporate Audit," Manila, 1986.
121. The American Chamber of Commerce in the Philippines has sought to demonstrate statistically its significant contributions to social development (in health programs, education, the arts, etc.) and in technology transfer programs, but with little impact on public opinion. *Ibid.*
122. *NYT* September 1, 1987.
123. Juan Concepcion, "Ongpin Eyes Standstill Option," *Manila Bulletin,* November 16, 1986.
124. The arrangement made with Mexico at the end of 1987 to issue new bonds, backed by U.S. bonds, to reduce its bank debt may have some application in the Philippines, though that arrangement was not as successful as hoped and involved an input of Mexican government money that Manila cannot match. *NYT* December 30 and 31, 1987.
125. On the Philippine view of the importance of the bases to Tokyo, see Jesus Bigornia, "Clark and Subic Have Their Own Value to Japan," *Manila Bulletin,* November 11, 1986.
126. At the end of the ASEAN summit meeting in Manila during December 1987, Japan's Prime Minister promised the leaders of all six countries a loan and investment package totaling $2 billion, as well as wider market access to Japan. Thus more help will be coming to the Philippines. *NYT* December 16, 1987.
127. Author's interview in Manila with former local official, November 18, 1986.

128. As noted earlier, Manila wishes to change the BLA and have Philippine labor law apply in the facilities, a step the U.S. strenuously opposes. FBIS, "Labor Terms Precondition for Base Talks," December 2, 1987.
129. Interview with former local official, November 18, 1986.
130. Donald E. Weatherbee surveys ASEAN security efforts with a skeptical view of an extensive military undertaking in "ASEAN: Patterns of National and Regional Resilience," Khil Young Whan and Lawrence E. Grinter, eds. *Asian–Pacific Security* (Boulder, CO: Lynne Rienner Publishers, 1986) pp. 201–223.
131. The early stages of SEANWFZ are discussed by Kavi Chongkittavorn in *The Nation* (Bangkok), February 18 and April 28, 1987.
132. See, for example, comments by Malaysian Prime Minister Mahathir Mohammed, who recognized "the need for the region to have something to balance out what the Russians have in Cam Ranh Bay and Danang." FBIS, "Paper Comments on ASEAN Summit Agenda," December 8, 1987.
133. Indonesia's then Foreign Minister Mokhtar Kusumaatmaja, in response to the Manglapus probe for ASEAN backing of the U.S.–Philippine base arrangement, said that it was impossible to support the idea. FBIS, "Mokhtar on U.S. Bases in the Philippines," October 23, 1987.
134. FBIS, "Additional Remarks on Bases," December 15, 1987.
135. *NYT* December 16, 1987.
136. In the fall of 1987, Thailand and Singapore emphasized the value of the bases and favored continuation of the U.S.–Philippines security relationship. On Thai Foreign Ministry attitudes see FBIS, "Paper on ASEAN, U.S. Bases," November 9, 1987; on Singapore, FBIS, "Paper Calls for Retention of U.S. Bases," November 16, 1987. Australia's Defense Minister Kim Beazley also weighed in with strong support of the U.S. facilities in the Philippines, FBIS, "Defense Minister on U.S. Bases in Philippines," November 23, 1987.
137. Foreign Secretary Raul Manglapus expressed a prevailing ASEAN view when he stated, "If one asks the Japanese to protect itself (sic) and extend its protection to its sealanes . . . then they would have to patrol all the way down to the Straits of Malacca, and that is something that the region is not yet ready for." FBIS, "Manglapus on Japan, U.S. Defense of Area," November 10, 1987.
138. Author's interview in Tokyo with informed Japanese, June 2, 1987.
139. TIAS 4509.
140. Author's interview in Tokyo with Japanese defense analyst, June 1, 1987.
141. Japan's former Foreign Minister Kosaka Zentaro, while in Manila, noted that the removal of the bases would create a vacuum "which would require Japan to come in and fill that vacuum." FBIS, "Japan's Kosaka Defends Pressure on U.S. Bases," November 18, 1987. More generally,

Nishihara Masashi estimates that "because of concern over the growing Soviet military power, Japan may grow to become a local actor in a military sense." "Japan's Political and Security Role in the Asian–Pacific Region," *Foreign Relations Journal,* January 1986, Vol. 1, no. 1, p. 54.
142. *NYT* December 17, 1987.

Part Two

U.S.–Philippine Bases Agreement: Looking to the Future

Conference Record
First Day: Tuesday, February 16, 1988
Origins of the Study
The Conference was informed that the Philippine Council for Foreign Relations originally initiated a study on U.S. Military Facilities in the Philippines as part of an effort to assist the Philippine Government in identifying and defining the principles and issues that need to be addressed in arriving at a decision on the future of those facilities. The PCFR thanked The Asia Foundation and the New York Council on Foreign Relations for hosting the conference "U.S.–Philippine Bases Agreement: Looking to the Future" that would allow a frank exchange of perceptions and ideas among Filipino and American scholars concerned with the objective and rational treatment of a subject of critical importance to Philippine–American relations.

Alliance Principles: Mutuality and Balance—Philippine Views
The opening session began with a broad discussion of the issues involved in the U.S. military facilities in the Philippines and the overall U.S.–Philippine security relationship. However, attention to fundamental principles was interwoven with discussion of specific aspects of the relationship in considering both the 1988 five-year review of the functioning of the 1947 Military Bases Agreement (MBA) and the subsequent negotiation of arrangements for the period after 1991, when the fixed term of the MBA comes to an end.

On the broad level, a Philippine participant argued that the MBA is part of an alliance between unequal partners and that the starting point for consideration of the future base relationship must be the principles of alliance, including a clear and precise statement of the premises underlying that relationship. The Philippine participant stressed that these premises must be mutually consistent, otherwise the details will degrade the objectives, and that the legitimacy and relevance of these premises must be re-examined under changed circumstances. The participant felt that, although the MBA was ostensibly based upon mutuality of interests and designed to promote the security interests of both countries, the concepts, in fact, had not been clearly defined from the outset and, from a Philippine standpoint, had never been balanced. Consequently, the MBA is not relevant or responsive to present Philippine needs and priorities.

The participant asserted that mutuality and parity of advantages were absent from the start, when the U.S. drafted the MBA without consultation with the Philippines. This is seen in all the provisions of the MBA, which focus on the use of the facilities by the U.S. and on Philippine obligations to ensure such use, without reference to a balance of advantages to be derived by the Philippines. As early as 1946 Philippine leaders had tried in vain to correct the one-sided nature of the arrangement.

This Philippine participant also observed that the U.S. and Philippine concepts of security and the basic philosophy and approach to national and regional security were apparently not congruent. The participant said that while U.S. defines security in terms of possession of military strength and defense, Philippine security is defined as "the satisfaction of values, which, on the national level pertain to the territorial integrity and well-being of the people." Military strength is only one of the strategies for security and should not be mistaken for the goal. As a small state, the Philippines must seek its security through friendly relations with other countries, emphasizing mutual respect for sovereignty. This is exemplified by the country's membership in ASEAN, which advocates peaceful coexistence and proposes the establishment of the Zone of Peace, Freedom and Neutrality (ZOPFAN). Moreover, the Philippines is primarily concerned with internal insurgency problems, while the U.S. focus is largely on regional and global problems. Forty years experience with the MBA has not enhanced Philippine security or military readiness but rather has created psychological insecurity and an attitude of dependence. The Filipino participant felt that the Philippine government has been denied even the freedom to decide who the enemy is, and that the problem is compounded because the U.S. notion of the enemy keeps changing. (Another participant said U.S. reliability against any enemy is questionable, in any case, in light of its having accepted stalemate in Korea and defeat in Vietnam.) It is necessary not only to define clearly what constitutes a threat and who the enemy is, but also to decide who should make those determinations.

Sovereignty was a major concern to this Philippine participant, who averred that certain provisions of the MBA and some aspects of the way U.S. facilities are operated greatly infringe on Philippine sovereignty. Specific examples were cited including: the "unhampered operations" provision in the MBA including U.S. control over movements in Subic Bay; limitations on Philippine exercise of criminal jurisdiction; non-operation of Philippine laws inside the bases; the U.S. right to use all Philippine roads, bridges, and other facilities; the need for U.S. consent for Filipinos to have access to or to utilize certain areas and natural resources located inside the bases; and American exploitation of natural reserves in the watershed—a right, the participant asserted, reserved only for Philippine citizens. The participant noted that while the MBA specifies the use of the facilities only for defense against external attacks in the "Pacific area," the facilities are now substantially, if not primarily, used to project U.S. presence in Northeast Asia (which this speaker considered outside the "Pacific area"), the Middle East, the Persian Gulf, and the Indian Ocean, thereby violating the provisions of the MBA. The participant also claimed the Philippines is denied knowledge of possible nuclear deployments in its own territory, despite the provisions of the new constitution barring all such weapons, because of the U.S. policy of neither denying nor confirming existence of such armaments in the facilities. The Philippine participant then stated that this will be a critical factor in the forthcoming five-year review. The participant said that while the Philippines recognizes that there is no absolute sovereignty in the world, any constraints on the country's sovereignty should be balanced by benefits. In the eyes of Filipinos, infringements on the country's sovereignty arising from the MBA have not been offset by corresponding and proper benefits and advantages.

The Philippine participant approached the issue of compensation as something paid for a commodity or service being rendered and said that it should not be tied up with any explicit or implicit demands from the source of the payment. The bases serve the interests of the United States, and the Philippines must therefore be compensated. The participant said that compensation should be distinct from aid, which other nations without U.S. facilities are also given. Further, expenditures related to operation of the bases should not be counted as part of compensation.

Finally, while acknowledging that some sectors have economically benefited from the existence of U.S. military facilities in the country, the participant stressed that social costs have also been high and affect not only those who reside near the bases but the greater part of the population. Beyond political or economic sensitivities, those social costs include creation of a sense of insecurity that pervades the soul of the people.

American Views

American participants agreed with the importance of mutuality for sustaining an alliance. They also agreed that the most immediate threats facing the Philippines are internal. However, American participants argued that by providing a secure external environment, which fostered economic and political development, and by extending military assistance in the form of equipment and training to deal with the communist insurgency as well as the Moslem secessionist movement, the relationship indeed provides mutual security and a balance of benefits. Furthermore, American participants stressed that the U.S. facilities also serve mutual interests as part of a global network contributing to deterrence of aggression.

American participants disputed the validity of the notion that the U.S. has frequently "changed enemies," pointing out that, rather than opposing a particular adversary, the American objective in Asia since the late nineteenth century has been to protect an "open system" in which each country can develop to its full potential in peace and stability. In this perspective, an American participant claimed, the United States and the Philippines have almost a total community of interests. American participants also challenged the charge of American unreliability in the defense of its allies, citing the postwar record of steadfastness in Europe and Asia, even in the face of domestic pressures after Vietnam to retreat to greater unilateralism or even isolationism.

Nonetheless, as the discussion progressed, some American participants cautioned that despite the strong desire in the U.S. to maintain and strengthen bilateral ties with the Philippines, including specifically the base relationship, given the current budget stringency in the

United States, and given the continuing concerns over political stability and communist insurgency in the Philippines, American flexibility in the base negotiations will not be infinite. Some American participants said that especially if there is a continuing easing of the international climate, whatever military planners may prefer in considering "worst case" contingencies, the political receptivity in the United States toward heavy outlays for overseas bases and toward accepting onerous terms for their maintenance will be affected. The recent cutoff of aid to Spain was cited in this context.

American participants were understanding of the importance of the sovereignty issue. However, they said that in meeting this legitimate Philippine concern, it was important not to pose unnecessary and debilitating obstacles to operations at the facilities that could undermine the effectiveness of the U.S. deterrent. In this respect, they emphasized that the U.S. policy of neither confirming nor denying the presence of nuclear weapons must be maintained. Finally, some American participants suggested that consideration of the criminal jurisdiction issue must take into account not only the Philippine need to exercise sovereignty but also the American obligation to protect its citizens, which is also a factor in the identical arrangements with Japan and NATO.

A Future Agreement

The Conference spent some time discussing the form an agreement might take on continued U.S. access to military facilities in the Philippines after 1991.

Philippine participants said the 1987 constitution mandates their government to take steps toward effecting a termination of the MBA in 1991. They maintained that although the constitution did not intend to dictate to the U.S. the form of any agreement governing U.S. access to the bases after 1991, it directs the Philippine government to negotiate a treaty. Some Philippine participants opined that the constitutional provision on this subject articulates a long-standing and deeply felt frustration over perceived inequalities in the MBA and the failure of the Philippine government to correct such conditions in past negotiations. A participant emphasized that if a new agreement were not considered, the decision-making process would be encumbered by an agreement dictated by circumstances prevailing forty years ago. Moreover, by putting any new agreement in the form of a treaty, the U.S. Congress as well as the administration would be committed to its terms.

American participants pointed out that the U.S. Supreme Court has ruled that an executive agreement has the same force in law as a treaty. They also explained that treaties are much more difficult to process through Congress and that the legislative branch has been deeply involved in—and thus committed to—all executive agreements since the late 1970s. They further explained that a treaty will not necessarily serve to commit Congress to appropriate specific sums over multiyear periods. In addition, they stressed that the involvement of the House of Representatives in the executive agreement process was a distinct benefit since the House originates all money bills (whereas the House has no formal role in the treaty process).

The Filipinos insisted that the constitutional mandate for a treaty reflected deep-seated feelings and suggested that it would be preferable for the conference to focus on substantive issues rather than on form. Although one Philippine participant said that the constitution required a treaty and not an agreement with the "status" of a treaty, whether an executive agreement could be construed to meet the Philippine legal requirement was left unresolved. The political importance of the U.S. accommodating the treaty requirement was, however, underscored by the Filipinos.

Compensation

The level and form of compensation was another principal focus of the discussion.

A Philippine participant said that the principle of U.S. payment of "compensation"—or whatever it is called—is not an issue; such payments have been made under the 1979 amendments to the MBA and as a result of the 1983 review. Furthermore, he stated that the U.S. is paying compensation to other countries that host what may be argued are less important bases. In reaching an agreement, the participant suggested that the U.S. consider the strategic value of the Philippine location and the historical ties between the two countries. One also needs to take into account other factors and terms affecting the existence and operations of the facilities such as command structure, ownership of the facilities, privileges, and exemptions from Philippine laws extended to U.S. forces and other parties in the facilities. Terms and arrangements the U.S. has entered into with other countries should be points of comparison. The necessity of such payments for the Philippine economy should also be a consideration.

Other Philippine participants considered that the amounts presently provided to the Philippines are grossly inadequate, particularly when compared with amounts paid to other countries with U.S. bases or even to countries in the Middle East without U.S. bases. They also argued that payment of compensation in the form of aid was unacceptable and complained that the process gives the U.S. leverage to interfere in internal Philippine affairs. Philippine participants insisted that compensation should take the form of unfettered rent for the use of the facilities. The present compensation scheme, which involves the U.S. president's "best effort" pledge to obtain funding from the Congress, is susceptible to congressional whim; therefore the amount of compensation, its line-item allocation, and the timing of its availability are unreliable. The shifting of funds from military aid to economic aid at the end of the Marcos presidency was cited to illustrate the point.

Americans noted that the Philippine demand for greater compensation comes at a time when the United States faces a severe budgetary squeeze. They pointed out that, nonetheless, and notwithstanding cuts in amounts given to other aid recipients in FY 88, the request for aid to the Philippines was not only not reduced by the Congress but was even increased. However, a number of American participants predicted the level of compensation in the future will be closely related to the duration and other aspects of post-1991 arrangements.

In connection with the discussion of the political and technical impediments to multiyear commitments of funds, an American participant recounted that, in fact, the amounts given by the U.S. to the Philippines exceeded figures stipulated in the president's "best effort" pledge. Specifically, the American participant indicated that between FY 85 and FY 88, the United States will have provided Economic Support Funds (ESF) in excess of $730 million as against $380 million expected under the "best effort" pledge. With military aid amounting to over $367 million (versus $340 million pledged), the total assistance of $1.1 billion for this period will exceed the promised amount by close to $400 million. The American participant also called attention to the fact that the grant component of military aid as delivered was almost 90 percent, even though in the original schedule military credits exceeded grants by more than 2:1. (All the ESF is grant aid.) It was also noted that this compensation package does not include $90 million in development assistance and support for land reform provided separately in FY 88.

Some American participants explained that the shifting of funds from military to economic aid at the end of the Marcos era represented, in part, a sympathetic American response to strong lobbying in Washington by Filipino oppositionists. In any case, an American participant pointed out that the agreed distribution of money between military and economic aid was stipulated over a five-year period rather than annually, and that any shortfall in notional levels of military assistance after 1983 had been made up for in the past two years since President Aquino had been in office. The same participant also explained that as for the issue of "rent" versus "aid," neither the president nor the Congress would provide funds without accountability to American taxpayers. In the American view, satisfactory implementation depends more on the state of relations between the two countries than on the formal nature of the arrangement. In that respect, both the U.S. performance and the tremendous reservoir of American goodwill toward the Philippines were cited as important indicators.

While acknowledging the points made by their American counterparts, Philippine participants nevertheless stated that the perception of Filipinos is that the U.S. manipulated the implementation of the compensation arrangements to American advantage. In considering factors that will affect support in the Philippines for any new arrangement, they underscored the importance of generating a favorable public perception, including a sense that the benefits are in balance.

Security and Deterrence

Philippine participants asked for a more detailed discussion of the concept of deterrence in order to understand how the very broad regional and global security concerns of the U.S. and the more focused Philippine national defense and security interests fit. Both sides agreed with the objective of maintaining an open system in Asia. However, the Philippines wanted to ensure that in the pursuit of this objective, national sovereignty and security were not compromised. In looking to the future of the U.S. facilities in their country, Filipinos needed to appreciate the gravity and extent of threats to their independence and territorial sovereignty over the next ten years, and also to determine how the American presence would reduce or aggravate such threats. Members of the Philippine delegation believed that Filipinos would only approve an agreement that they perceived as both contributing significantly to the security of the country and, at the same time, preserving national sovereignty.

A Filipino participant said that foreign military presence in any country is an anachronism and is an affront to the dignity and sovereignty of an independent nation. It may only be justified if it more fully protects the overall independence and sovereignty of the host country.

He said that "assuming away" the U.S. military presence would not be easy, and in view of the lack of plans for withdrawal, its continuation seems assured. But the form and terms of such presence should be carefully analyzed and defined. One issue was whether land and water form part of the "facilities." A clear definition of the possible employment of the U.S. forces at the facilities needs to be specified in the agreement; this would both justify and limit the U.S. use of the facilities. The Philippine participant said that what privileges and immunities will be granted, and to whom, must be specified in great detail to avoid abuse and minimize perceived discrimination against Filipinos.

The Philippine participant maintained that any U.S. military presence in the country after 1991 would most likely be for a relatively brief period and that any agreement should be viewed as looking to a phasing out. He said that many Filipinos believe the facilities constitute a magnet for either a conventional or, more serious, a nuclear attack.

These apprehensions needed to be weighed against potential benefits. Philippine participants hoped Americans would realize that what must be addressed in many of these areas are not only material issues but emotional ones as well.

American participants responded that along with the very important bilateral relationship and commitments, the United States necessarily views the facilities in the context of its regional and global responsibilities. They said that it is very important to the U.S. that Filipinos understand and appreciate those responsibilities. They noted that all basing relationships present problems—some quite difficult—that need to be addressed seriously. But, they said, there needs to be an appreciation on both sides of why we are working together and a mechanism to adjust constructively as the situation changes. Americans cannot believe that Philippine leaders do not understand U.S. responsibilities. In contrast to views expressed by Filipinos at this conference about derogation of sovereignty created by the facilities, many other host nations would consider their sovereignty weakened if the U.S. withdrew.

As for the use of the facilities in ways potentially detrimental to Philippine interests, some American participants cited Washington's respect for Manila's sensitivities in conducting the Vietnam war. They observed that the U.S. record around the world in responding to concerns and sensitivities of host nations in this regard has been virtually impeccable.

Some American participants observed that assistance provided under the MBA bolstered Philippine efforts to deal with a serious and unresolved communist insurgency problem and Moslem insurrection. Philippine armed forces received badly needed equipment and training that helped to deal with these problems as well as to overcome certain aspects of the failure of the Philippine government to deal effectively with the armed forces. They said the U.S. presence has also substantially reduced the budgetary and financial burden of the Philippine government in providing for external security needs.

Some Philippine participants, however, expressed the belief that the communist threat is well on the way to resolution, citing results of polls showing a clear decline in public support for insurgents in the countryside. They also said that there had recently been substantial improvements in the relationship between the military and the civilian government as well as in military cohesiveness and morale. Other Philippine participants disagreed with this optimistic assessment of the insurgency situation but cautioned that the U.S. should not become actively involved in the fighting; Filipinos prefer to win this conflict by themselves as the Thai had done. American participants emphasized that while the U.S. had not fought in place of the Thais, it nevertheless had provided substantial material and other assistance that the Thais needed to win.

With respect to the Mutual Defense Treaty, several participants on both sides felt that the MDT could survive a withdrawal of the U.S. facilities but that it would likely need to be reviewed in light of the changed situation. A Philippine participant speculated that if the Philippines could remain under the "umbrella" of the MDT, removal of the MBA would enhance the Philippine sense of independence, sovereignty, dignity and respect and might make the two countries better allies. Another indicated that if the Philippines were not host to U.S.

facilities, reaching a consensus in the Philippines on the U.S. regional role would be easier. Foreshadowing more extensive discussion on the subject during the next day, a Philippine participant said it was necessary to address provisions in the MBA for the phase-out of the U.S. facilities, including what equipment should remain and what should be removed.

American and Filipino participants referred to the view of ASEAN nations, Japan, and other Asian countries on the future of U.S. facilities in the Philippines. Americans felt that most, if not all, of those nations highly value the U.S. presence and consider it important to their security. It was recalled that when the U.S. considered withdrawing from the region in the wake of the defeat in Vietnam, many Asian nations implored the U.S. to remain. Several of the nations were concerned that if the United States moved out of the region, Japan would increase its military strength and expand its security role in Southeast Asia.

Some Philippine participants acknowledged that despite pronouncements of some countries that they ultimately want to have the region free from superpower involvement, U.S. presence is actually welcomed by a number of nations. For their own part, however, and considering the interests of the Philippines, the participants drew a distinction between the general issue of U.S. "presence" in the region and the specific issue of the military facilities continuing in the Philippines.

An American reiterated the U.S. focus on maintaining an open system in Asia. Security is but one component of a set of balanced interests that includes economic development, emigration, the fostering of regional organizations such as ASEAN, and sustaining democratic values. The Philippines must ask itself, he said, if it benefits from this system and if it wants it to continue.

As participants looked forward to the second day of the Conference, they kept in mind three basic options on the future of the U.S. military facilities that were identified on the first day:

- continued operation of the facilities, albeit with some modifications in the arrangements;
- continued U.S. access to the facilities under significantly altered arrangements;
- U.S. withdrawal from the facilities.

Second Day, Wednesday, February 17, 1988

The Role of the Facilities—An American Perspective

An American participant observed that the most difficult negotiations for a U.S. ambassador often take place not with foreign governments but in Washington, where the ambassador must try to introduce into the foreign policymaking process attitudes and realities in other countries that may run counter to U.S. policies and perceptions. Understanding the attitudes and decision-making process in Washington is important for any party intending to undertake negotiations with the U.S. Specific to the forthcoming negotiations on U.S. Military Facilities in the Philippines, the participant stressed that it would be tragic if the relationship of the two countries were to suffer because one or both sides misread the perceptions, priorities, and limitations of the other: that is, the Philippine concern for national security and sovereignty, on the one hand, and the U.S. global responsibilities, on the other.

The American participant said that the U.S. government prefers the status quo, as change will require it to examine the interplay of vested interests, budget, and conflicting priorities as well as perceptions of the political, bureaucratic, and congressional elements involved.

He added that Americans do not readily recognize that other governments and leaders also have internal political problems. The speaker stressed that Washington's concerns are global and are based on the belief that the U.S. has a world mission to preserve and protect freedom and democracy. He noted that the U.S. has frequently taken risks and made sacrifices for that cause. Washington, therefore, expects that those who benefit from U.S. support will accept its view of its mission.

Washington, he said, views the Philippine bases as much, if not more, in a regional and global context as in a Philippine context. Citing congressional testimony by then Assistant Secretary of State Paul Wolfowitz in 1983, the speaker said that the U.S. facilities in the Philippines are regarded as evidence of the "abiding commitment" of the U.S. to the Philippines under the Mutual Defense Treaty. At the same time, however, the facilities also play a crucial role in U.S. efforts to provide an effective counterbalance in the area to the growing military power of the Soviet Union and its surrogates, to support U.S. treaty commitments in East Asia, to strengthen ties with ASEAN, to protect the sea and air lanes in an area important to world trade, and to provide logistic support for U.S. forces in the Indian Ocean and Southwest Asia designed to maintain peace and stability.

U.S. military facilities in the Philippines have strategic value for Northeast Asia, Southeast Asia, and the Indian Ocean. Today, the strategic importance of the Philippine bases centers on their support of the U.S. role and presence in the Persian Gulf and the Middle East. Nonetheless, even though in the proximate Northeast and Southeast Asia areas the strategic importance of the facilities is related more to conjectured contingencies than to immediate threats, the United States still sees itself as a significant power in Asia and has treaty obligations and implied commitments whose implementation would be significantly affected by the elimination of its presence in the Philippines. In light of this fact, the public attitudes of these countries toward the facilities have not been expressed as clearly as Washington would like.

The strategic view of Americans on the bases is based on a series of assumptions:

- U.S. bases are important to all areas for symbolic as well as operational reasons. Despite public professions of a preference that both superpowers leave, Americans believe people in the region look to the U.S. for their ultimate security. Thus, the departure of the U.S. from the Philippines would create a strategic imbalance in the area, creating subtle momentum toward political accommodation with other protectors and raising troubling questions about Japan's future role in the region.
- Notwithstanding the Filipino desire to have a greater voice in how the facilities are to be used, the Philippine government and people accept the wider regional and global role of the facilities.
- Japan and Korea attach major significance to the continued existence of U.S. military facilities in the Philippines.
- Although ASEAN countries are inhibited from publicly expressing their support for the facilities, the U.S. has no reason to believe they oppose the continued U.S. presence.
- Countries in the Indian Ocean welcome cooperation in Asia, as symbolized by the Philippine bases, which will allow the U.S. to respond to contingencies in their area.

Ironically, the American speaker said, the greater reluctance with respect to the U.S. continuing to play a global or regional peacekeeping role may be found in Washington itself. Though it has not been reluctant to use its power if the objective was clear and the action relatively short, historically the U.S. has been apprehensive about foreign commitments. The Vietnam experience aggravated the inhibitions. However, the American people continue to support maintenance of bases abroad in the recognition that the global competition between the United States and the Soviet Union has not ended.

At the same time, he said, Americans are asking whether the new situation in the Soviet Union and changes since the end of the Second World War do not require a rethinking of global strategy, including a greater sharing of the burden by America's allies. Arguments over deficits and government expenditures feed these questions.

The U.S. remains proud and strong and wishes to maintain its global role, but a feeling exists that America cannot do it all, and others who share the concerns of Americans over democracy and freedom are expected to do their part. As the Spanish people have found, pressures for reduction or elimination of a U.S. strategic presence are not likely to be well received in Washington, and no nation should assume that the U.S. will be willing to pay any price to retain a facility.

The American participant concluded by asking whether a formula for the facilities can be found that combines the Philippine interest about national security and sovereignty with U.S. global responsibilities. To this end, he suggested the following approaches:

- The nearing of 1991 and the requirements of the Philippine Constitution should cause both countries to positively examine their priorities and perceptions in the field of security.
- The U.S. should attempt to formulate a more precise and confidence-building statement on its role in the defense of the Philippines.
- The U.S. must recognize and address Philippine apprehensions over possible vulnerability created for the country by the U.S. global role, perhaps through a commitment for continuing high-level consultations.
- The Philippines should, in turn, recognize that U.S. presence not only relieves the government of part of the burden of national defense but also maintains an important security balance in the region.
- Both sides need to examine together the most feasible and effective instruments to express American commitments with respect to the facilities, taking account of the clear Philippine desire that such commitments be expressed in the form of a treaty or its

equivalent(s). Treaties, executive agreements, and joint resolutions of Congress were cited as possible instruments.

The speaker underscored the importance of Philippine security to the United States and the need to match that objective with broader U.S. responsibilities.

Philippine Perspectives

A Filipino participant said that the preceding American presentation greatly contributed to the better understanding of the U.S. concerns. The participant noted the understandable preference of the U.S. government for the status quo, as compared with the Filipino desire for rectification of certain provisions in the arrangements, if not termination. Perhaps, he said, the issue is not ultimate objectives, but rather how to identify and accommodate objectives and concerns of each party and make them compatible. If Filipinos are to remain involved, he said, it would be most helpful if they could be assisted to understand better what U.S. global responsibilities really are, what the security balance precisely necessitates, and how this is linked to democracy in the Philippines. He expressed interest in sharing at a leadership level, for example, what the U.S. predictions are about possible future actions by the Soviet Union, China, India, and other countries. At the same time, Americans need to be aware of Philippine concerns, some of which may be emotional, and to update arrangements in the context of those concerns.

The Filipino also called attention to the fact that procedural issues, or how an arrangement might be reached, are as important as substantive issues and, therefore, equally need to be looked into. The key is goodwill and understanding. The speaker stressed that it is most important that, if the U.S. has to finally leave the Philippines (as it most probably would at some time in the future), such a departure should take place under friendly and mutually acceptable circumstances. It would be a tragedy for the U.S. just to pick up and go.

"Nuclear Magnet"

Referring to the "nuclear magnet" issue raised on the first day, a member of the Philippine delegation said that with the concept of limited nuclear war adopted toward the end of the Carter administration, and with the American refusal to pledge "no first use" of nuclear weapons, Filipinos saw the U.S. presence in the Philippines as part of a first-strike capability, and the facilities thus as a primary nuclear target. He asked how one might answer such concerns.

The American delegation said it foresaw no scenario in which the U.S. facilities in the Philippines would involve the country in an isolated nuclear attack. Bases in the Philippines do not have any quick strike capability against the Soviet Union and therefore do not fit into any first-strike scenario. American forces in the Philippines are designed to strike regional targets, not the Soviet Union. As such, if there ever were an attack on the facilities in the Philippines, it would come in the context of an already worldwide confrontation in which all of mankind would be way down the road to mutual destruction. Even if the U.S. facilities were no longer present, some Americans felt the bases might well be attacked in a general war in order to prevent the U.S. from moving back in. (Others did not foresee the use of nuclear weapons, or even substantial conventional weapons, against the facilities, since their operation could be impeded through minimal blocking actions. In this way, the Soviets would preserve the facilities for their own future use.)

Several Filipino participants expressed the view that the facilities would become a target for nuclear or conventional attack if war broke out on any scale, whereas without the facilities, even in the case of a general nuclear war, the Philippines would be spared. As one Philippine participant put it, for the U.S. the issue is one of military victory; for the Philippines the issue is the suffering of the people and national survival: "We are more interested in preserving the country."

Deterrence

The Conference proceeded to discuss the U.S. strategy of deterrence.

The American side explained that the U.S. objective is to prevent a war, not fight one, but that the strategy of deterrence is based on the belief that the most effective way to avoid a conflict is to be prepared for one. This strategy requires the U.S. to maintain high visibility and credibility of its capability and willingness to fight. It is the danger and risk that this war-fighting capability presents that will restrain adversary from launching an attack. American participants further explained that the strategy of deterrence is important in the conduct of foreign diplomacy in preventing any party from exercising nuclear blackmail against other countries. The U.S. military facilities in the Philippines are part of an interdependent global network of alliance relationships and strategic facilities among countries that share certain values and ways of life they want to preserve and that they feel can be better protected by standing together. When certain alliance partners start to view their defense concerns individually, resulting in a decision to pull out of the network of relationships, deterrence is significantly weakened. To be effective, deterrence must be able to count on mutuality in the defense systems and the willingness of participating parties to maintain the combat credibility of the whole network.

To Deal with Which Threat?
In response to a Filipino inquiry, American participants clarified that deterrence not only pertains to nuclear capability but also involves capability to respond to conventional conflicts. A Filipino participant reiterated concern over the need for a clear definition of exactly the sorts of situations or threats to Philippine security in which it may expect U.S. assistance. He referred to an incident in which, he charged, the U.S. refused not only to provide support but even to sell the Philippine government munitions needed to counter an invasionary attack that took place some years back in Mindanao by some Filipinos trained by a neighboring country and—he asserted—assisted by troops from that country. This incident reinforced Filipino perceptions of the great gap between American commitments to Philippine national defense and American concern for maintaining its regional and global roles. Filipinos said that history tends to prove that the U.S. military facilities have not been meaningful and effective in preventing or responding to smaller types of national defense conflicts or threats with which developing countries like the Philippines are more likely to get entangled.

American participants did not argue the facts of the "incident" described, which are at variance with the understanding of the United States, but some said that the U.S. is committed only to defending the "Metropolitan Philippines" and would not want to get involved in border conflicts or matters concerning contested territories. In addition, an American participant questioned to what extent the Philippine government really wants the U.S. to get involved in internal conflicts. This led the Filipino participants to refer back to questions raised during discussions in the first day of the conference about what constitutes and who defines a threat. A Filipino participant judged that the U.S. has generally been reluctant to get involved in Philippine defense problems where the threats are not from communists. Members of the

Philippine delegation insisted that, as illustrated by the incident cited, the lack of congruence between the Filipino and American perceptions over priorities among national, regional and global defense interests underscores that these areas require precise definition and that they need to be carefully considered in examining the bases agreement and in reaching a decision about its future.

At the start of the afternoon session, an American participant again stressed that the U.S. views deterrence as based on preventing war, not fighting one. He added that an outbreak of a nuclear war was not likely to start with a direct Soviet attack on the U.S. but would most likely arise out of a crisis in an area where the interests of the U.S. and the Soviet Union were not clear and where one side misjudged the interests of the other and precipitated a crisis. In this context, he opined, the U.S. facilities in the Philippines represent a clear statement of U.S. determination—of its will and capability—to maintain peace and security in the whole of Asia.

The U.S. believes the Soviet Union has posed a threat since World War II, and most of the world agrees, this participant said. He continued that it is not yet possible to project the effects on Soviet foreign relations of internal policy changes taking place in the Soviet Union. Even if such changes were to be ultimately reflected in Soviet foreign policy, he added, it is still too early to reduce alertness and tempt the Soviet Union with irresistible opportunities. In explaining why U.S. military facilities in the Philippines are so important, attention was drawn to the fact that Asian countries have not developed the sense of community that their European counterparts have. As a result, countries in Asia have not established a collective security system like the one that works well in Europe. Other factors that contribute to the importance of the facilities include the history of close relations between the two countries and the unique geographic location of the Philippines.

Balance of Benefits

The American speaker stated further that, notwithstanding the differences in size between the Philippines and the U.S. and in their contribution to their mutual defense arrangement, there is a parity of benefits between the two nations considering their common interest in preserving an open system in which countries can pursue their destinies free from outside pressure. This, he said, is perhaps the most important consideration that prevents the Philippines from becoming impartial in the U.S.-Soviet conflict. The speaker talked of potential consequences in the region if the U.S. were to withdraw, including possible Soviet intervention in the Philippines. He said this may seem farfetched, but the point is that it is too easy to assume nothing will change. Finally, the speaker said that while the U.S. military facilities in the Philippines are very important, they are not so vital that they cannot be compensated for militarily. The cost the U.S. government should be willing to pay for their continued use must, therefore, be less than the cost to relocate, considering the uncertainty regarding the position that future Philippine administrations might take over continuance or abrogation of the arrangement.

The speaker said that the possible psychological consequences of a U.S. withdrawal from the facilities for foreign investment and other economic factors is difficult to appreciate at this point. He was sure, however, that U.S. aid to the Philippines would be severely affected immediately if only because the U.S. government would need funds to pay for relocation. Other costs and adverse effects would likely become obvious over time. He suggested each country needed to be more understanding of the other's sensitivities in order to avoid the high costs for both of a breakdown.

U.S.-Philippine Economic Relations—A Philippine View

A Filipino presented the Conference with his observations on current trends in four areas of economic interaction between the Philippines and the U.S.: trade; investment; aid (loans and grants); and the direct economic impact of expenditures by the U.S. at the facilities.

He said that while the U.S. remains an important trading partner of the Philippines, its contribution to the total trade is declining. Specifically, whereas the U.S. accounted for 80 percent of Philippine trade in the 1940s, its share now fluctuates between 27 and 35 percent, and it is projected to stabilize at 25 to 30 percent in the future. The drop in the U.S. share of Philippine trade is the result of various factors, among which are the conscious effort of the Philippine government over the past two decades to diversify sources and destinations of the country's imports and exports as well as the declining competitiveness of U.S products in the Philippine domestic market. Protectionism has also led to a shrinkage of the U.S. market.

As in trade, although the contribution of American investments in the Philippines remains very large (some 57 percent in 1985–86), its contribution to the total inflow of foreign investment has been declining. Moreover, there is no specific pattern indicating that the presence of U.S. facilities in the country attracts American investments.

Loans and development assistance sourcing is also clearly shifting more and more to Japan, which is able to provide low-cost, long-term financing. In addition, he said, Japanese loans and development assistance are no longer predominantly tied to the purchase of goods and services from Japan and are increasingly directed toward budget-deficit financing. Europeans and Canadians are also increasing their contributions to the Philippine economy. U.S. aid is increasing, especially development assistance, but as a proportion of total aid to the Philippines it is losing relative importance.

Philippine GNP is officially estimated at $33 billion. A dynamic "underground economy," however, is estimated to contribute an additional 35 percent for a real total of about $45 billion (bringing per capita income closer to $1,000 than the official estimate of $550). On the other hand, the U.S. daily expenditures in the facilities are estimated at approximately $1 million. If the economy continues to grow in current terms at 15 to 16 percent a year, such expenditures could drop from their current 3 percent share of Gross Domestic Product to only 2 percent in six years. Projected over ten to fifteen years, that share would be minimal.

The presentation concluded that a 15-year phase-out of the facilities would provide enough time to cushion and moderate the adverse impact on the economy, including on the critical issue of employment. Utilization of areas presently occupied by the bases in more productive agricultural and industrial undertakings would provide good economic opportunities for people now in the communities surrounding the U.S. facilities.

Issues to Consider

An American participant enumerated eight issues that he suggested should be carefully examined in determining the future of the facilities:

- compensation
- criminal jurisdiction
- 1991 "expiration" date and the constitutional provisions
- form of agreement
- nuclear issue

- definition of U.S. commitment to Philippine security
- forms and content of a rent or aid package
- long-range security and military requirements and how they affect future understanding

Another American added "unhampered operations" to the list.

U.S.–Philippine Economic Relations—An American View

An American participant noted the impressive recovery and growth the Philippine economy is making at present. He agreed that there seems to be no correlation between the U.S. presence in Philippine bases and American investments in the country. He cited the fact that, while investors may take comfort in such a presence, and even though U.S. investors have been enjoying good returns on their equity in the Philippines, other countries without U.S. military facilities receive their share of American investments. Finally he pointed out that an important consideration for Filipinos to think about is the partnership between the two countries in the fight for greater openness in the world trading system. He stated that even as there has been a clamor in the U.S. Congress for trade restrictions, the U.S. remains one of the most open markets to Philippine exports. He cited the recent U.S. decision to withdraw preferential tariffs from four newly industrialized countries (NICs) in Asia (South Korea, Taiwan, Hong Kong, and Singapore) as providing the Philippines with excellent opportunities to expand nontraditional exports.

Domestic and International Military Considerations

The American participant also noted that the economic performance is a signal of significant stabilization since the last coup attempt in August 1987. Reacting to this point, a Filipino participant pointed out that while the coup was regrettable for creating some instability, it nonetheless provided a good opportunity for the present administration to correct a number of festering conditions affecting the relationship of the military with the civilian government, including rectification of what was perceived by some as a leftist bias on the part of President Aquino.

Returning to the broader aspects of the U.S. perception of the facilities, an American participant recalled that before the Vietnam War, the U.S. was drawing down in Asia. However, as a result of the Soviet buildup and assertive behavior in the area since then, U.S.

concern and interest has been reinvigorated and the Philippine bases have taken on a new value. This may be uncomfortable for the Philippines, but the strategic picture is likely to remain as it is for some time.

Another American asked how the Philippines would really feel about significant changes in the U.S. presence in light of the potential Japanese role (including a substantially increased military role), growing PRC strength, and unknown Soviet intentions. He noted that a "terminal phase" of 20–25 years would have far different implications for the U.S. than a phase-out of a much shorter period. He also wondered whether giving up some of the facilities would help make continuation of others more bearable for Filipinos.

A Philippine participant responded with questions about what the U.S. would do in the event negotiations failed and what price the U.S. was willing to pay to make them succeed. This participant also raised the possibility of "staggered withdrawal."

Impact of a Changing International Environment

An American reflected that the continuation of U.S.–Philippine relations requires serious self-examination and the willingness of each party to keep an open and flexible attitude toward various issues. He pointed out that in the case of deterrence, particularly with respect to conventional deterrence, Americans need to stretch their minds seriously in deciding how much is enough and how it needs to be displayed. Beyond the domestic constraints already discussed, many people see rapid changes in the international environment that make it more difficult to reach such judgments. If the security environment seems less threatening, one needs to consider if the same level of deterrence is necessary. He specifically commented on the tendency of military planners to design forces based on the requirements of worst-case scenarios.

In the case of the Philippines, what is critical, he said, is not to do anything precipitous; one cannot make rash assumptions about what the international environment will look like in five years. The issue, he said, is whether to extend U.S. access to the facilities for a fixed period, holding open the option of renewal in case of developments that concern either or both parties, or whether we should negotiate an arrangement to phase out the facilities over an agreed period. He said that the U.S. must begin to accept Philippine realities, but the Philippines also needs to understand that the U.S. may be coming to grips with the fact that it is no longer the power it once was; the American ability to wield political influence and create a benign security environment may be shrinking. Phasing out over an agreed period could avoid an injurious reaction in the U.S. and a confrontation over potentially conflicting sovereign interests.

Another American said that it might be better to think in terms of an agreement that goes into the future but could be curtailed, rather than an agreement for a limited period that could be extended. He also cautioned that there would be a substantial difference in the U.S. reaction, including the terms acceptable in a new agreement, depending on how one defined "phasing out." If one meant less than ten years, much of what had been discussed in terms of U.S. flexibility, including on compensation, would be open to serious question.

Difficult Issues—Need for Openness and Flexibility

A Philippine participant suggested that Americans should be more creative in addressing the issue of compensation and in formulating possible schemes. One possible formulation to be examined was the one in the U.S. agreement with Micronesia, as mentioned in Professor Greene's paper. This model included American backing of its financial obligation with the "full faith and credit" of the United States. An American response to this suggestion was that, while the Micronesian model was worth considering, the Philippines should realize that the agreement contained many special features, including a long-term pledge by the territories to provide military access to the U.S., if Washington desired, while denying the same to the Soviet Union.

A Philippine participant said that in past negotiations, when the two countries really worked to reach agreement, goodwill and a spirit of accommodation had led both parties to be more specific and flexible in their requirements and more innovative in the manner of stating them. He called attention to the term "unhampered operations" that seemed to overstate the real U.S. needs at the cost of evoking an emotional response from the Philippines leading to a stalemate on the issue.

On the other side of the coin, another Philippine participant said that the situation is complicated enough without being dominated by ideas from the ASEAN neighbors. In this context, ZOPFAN is an unnecessary complication; the proposed Southeast Asia Nuclear Weapons Free Zone is even worse and ignores the reality of other nuclear powers such as China.

Most of the participants emphasized the importance of starting talks early in the light of the complexity of the issues and the likelihood that politics in both countries would contribute even more difficulties and delays. Both delegations also agreed on the need for candor and the willingness to listen to and really understand the concerns and sensitivities of the other side, how they think and why. Participants were unanimous in their acceptance that the effort in the Conference had been properly focused on identifying and illuminating issues and exchanging ideas on how they should be dealt with rather than in immediately reaching answers and solutions.

Finally, the Conference reaffirmed that Filipinos and Americans share fundamental values and that the key to preserving the close relationship between the two countries is the willingness to go an extra mile in understanding the problems and priorities as well as concerns and constraints of each side, in the interest of resolving differences with mutually satisfactory arrangements reached in a mutually acceptable way.

Philippine Council for Foreign Relations, Inc.
Council on Foreign Relations, Inc.

Bodega Bay, California
February 16–17, 1988

Part Three

U.S. Facilities in the Philippines

Alva M. Bowen, Jr.

Facilities at Clark Air Base and Subic Bay Naval Base in the Philippines support a peacetime U.S. military presence in Southeast Asia. In wartime they would support military operations in pursuit of U.S. objectives in East Asia and the Indian Ocean regions.

The potential benefits of the Philippines as a location for military bases figured prominently in the decision-making that led to the acquisition of those islands as an American colony in 1898. But whether the political and strategic costs of "fortifying" the Philippines are worth the benefits has been debated ever since.

To reassure the Japanese as part of the naval limitations agreement signed in Washington in 1922, the United States agreed not to fortify the Philippine islands. But when the agreement began to unravel in the mid-1930s, efforts to overcome the by then nearly defenseless condition of the islands proved too little and too late before war came in 1941.

Postwar policymakers in both the United States and the Philippines determined not to let that happen again, and they agreed that the United States would continue to maintain a base structure after Philippine independence in 1946.[1] This base structure was quite large at the end of the war, but over the years was reduced in both the number of separate installations and the amount of land reserved for use by the United States. Initially the bases were entirely under U.S. jurisdiction. This was formally changed in 1979 by an amendment to the bases agreement that explicitly stated that:

1. The bases are Philippine military bases over which Philippine sovereignty extends.

2. Each base shall be under the command of a Philippine base commander.
3. The United States shall have the use of certain facilities and areas within the bases and control over United States personnel, employees, equipment and materiel. Consistent with its rights and privileges under the 1947 agreement, as amended, the United States shall be assured unhampered military operations involving its forces in the Philippines.

By this amendment the U.S. "facilities" are now located on Philippine bases commanded by a Philippine officer subject to Philippine government control. These facilities comprise some of the real estate and most of the U.S.-made improvements (piers, buildings, runways, magazines, fuel depots etc.) encompassed within the former U.S. bases. The facilities are manned by U.S. servicemen and civilians and commanded by officers of the U.S. Armed Forces.

A 1983 successor amendment[2] added a commitment that the United States, notwithstanding the provision of the 1979 amendment assuring the United States of unhampered operations involving its forces in the Philippines, would consult with the government of the Philippines before:

1. using the bases for any combat operations other than those conducted in accordance with the Philippines–United States Mutual Defense Treaty or the Southeast Asian Collective Defense Treaty (Manila Pact), or;
2. establishment of long-range missiles in the bases.

These amendments to the bases agreement, negotiated with a Philippine government demonstrably friendly to the United States, nevertheless reflected some serious policy disagreements between the two governments that were resolved by restricting U.S. privileges.

A revolution in 1986 brought a different but still friendly government to power. The new government is still challenged by dissenters on the right and left who may not be as friendly to the United States if they gain control. To survive, the government may be required to further limit U.S. use of its facilities, raise the price for their continued use, or even withdraw access to the bases altogether when the fixed term of the bases agreement expires in 1991.[3]

This paper examines the functions presently fulfilled by the U.S. facilities and then analyzes options should conditions in the Philippines deteriorate and continued U.S. use of the facilities there become counterproductive.

Functions Fulfilled by U.S. Facilities in the Philippines

U.S. facilities in the Philippines support U.S. military forces stationed in Southeast Asia under the strategic principle of "forward defense" that has guided U.S. general purpose force planning since the late 1940s. This section presents the commonly accepted rationale for maintaining a permanent military presence in that region.

Purpose of a U.S. Military Presence in East Asia

The two major American goals for the Pacific Basin, as elsewhere, are continued access to valuable trading and resource areas and careful maintenance of the currently stable global strategic balance. Radical change in either the political or economic structure of the region might threaten both these goals. The term "stability," by which is meant the absence of radical, adverse political and economic change, is frequently used as shorthand for both goals. An underlying assumption, not always explicitly stated, is that "stability" is enhanced when foreign investors and local policymakers feel militarily secure.[4]

U.S. policymakers believe a U.S. military presence in East Asia supports these goals in two ways: politically, by reassuring friends and allies of our capability and willingness to use military force to meet treaty obligations and punish military adventurism we consider inimical to our interests; and militarily, by enabling prompt action when military intervention is chosen as the appropriate response to a crisis. Early intervention can minimize the military effort required.

At the global level, this "forward defense" in East Asia ensures the Soviets will have to plan for an Asian theater if they contemplate any military venture against the United States.

Since the end of World War II, despite some major dissent both from within and outside the various administrations, U.S. governments have consistently held that actually stationing U.S. military forces in East Asia is necessary. The official view has been that, while holding the same forces in the United States might provide some confidence among East Asians in the U.S. willingness to employ them to meet our Asian commitments, this would not be a satisfactory substitute for stationing U.S. military forces in visible positions in Korea, Japan, and the Philippines to counter immediately a border crossing in Korea or threats to the sea and air lanes needed for trade and strategic support of American friends and allies in the region.[5]

The Philippines in U.S. Security Planning

Despite occasional lapses, U.S. military forces have been based in the Philippines since the end of the nineteenth century and have come to be regarded as a fixture by policymakers in the region. The political effect of this fact is considerable but will not be further addressed in this paper. This section examines only the military benefits derived from the U.S. Philippine facilities.

Strategic Considerations. Geography divides East Asia strategically into two subregions, each with an enclosed sea formed by offshore archipelagos. U.S. military goals are different for each subregion.

The Northeast Asian subregion consists of the Sea of Japan, enclosed by the Japanese Islands and shared with them by the Soviets and Koreans on the mainland. Wartime U.S. strategic goals for Northeast Asia are to fulfill treaty obligations to Japan and the Republic of Korea, thereby keeping them and their industrial bases on our side, and to keep the Soviets from breaking out of the Sea of Japan.

The Southeast Asian subregion consists of the South China Sea, enclosed by Taiwan, the Philippines, Brunei, Malaysia, and Singapore and shared by them with the People's Republic of China, Vietnam, Thailand, Kampuchea, Malaysia, and Singapore on the mainland. Wartime U.S. strategic goals for Southeast Asia are: to keep the sea and air routes through the South China Sea and east of the Philippines open for our use and for the use of our friends and allies; to prevent our adversaries from using these routes; to fulfill treaty commitments to assist in defense of allies; and to keep China neutral or on our side.

Another U.S. strategic goal in wartime would be to keep open the sea and air routes from the U.S. mainland to the Japanese industrial base. The great circle route to Northeast Asia passes close to Soviet mainland bases and may be closed. A more southerly route, passing

U.S. Facilities in the Philippines 109

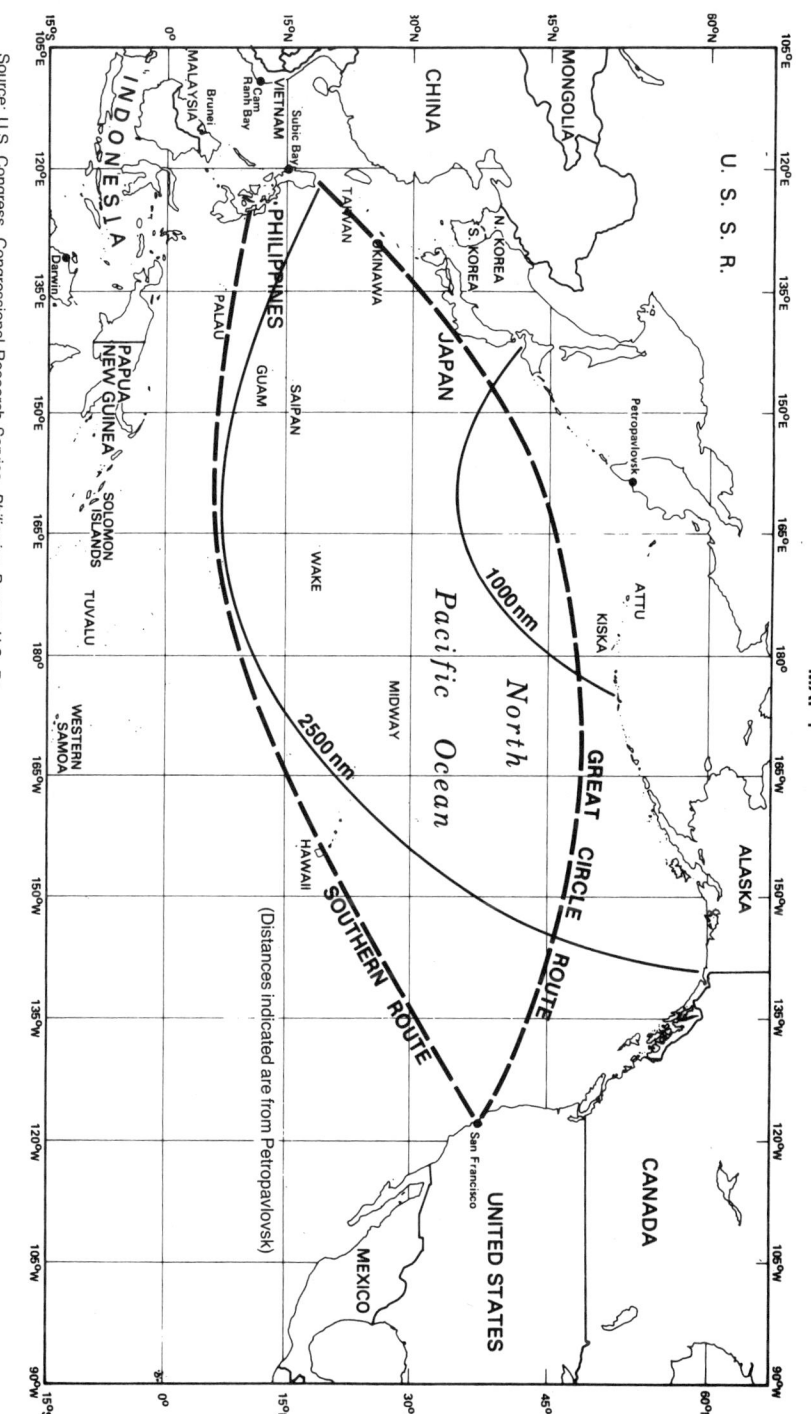

MAP 1

Source: U.S. Congress, Congressional Research Service, *Philippine Bases: U.S. Redeployment Options*, p. CRS 11. No. 86-44 F. February 20, 1986. The Library of Congress. Washington D.C. 1986.

near U.S. island bases including the Philippines, is safer. (See map 1.)

The Southeast Asian sea and air routes also provide a way through the land barrier between the Pacific and Indian Oceans. When U.S. security planners faced with supporting military operations in the region of the Persian Gulf compare the safety and reliability of routes through the Pacific with those via the Cape of Good Hope or Suez, the Pacific route often seems best because the Philippines provides a convenient way station for airlift aircraft on the long trip.

Soviet military presence in Vietnam complicates attainment of all these U.S. goals. Soviet bases in Vietnam threaten the safety of Southeast Asia's sea and air routes. These routes are vital to all the East Asian countries. Soviet forces in Vietnam could easily be augmented till they seem overwhelming to the modest defense forces of these countries.[6] Without offsetting U.S. forces China, Japan, and Korea might feel compelled to seek an accommodation with the Soviets to insure the safety of their commerce.

Capabilities and Missions of U.S. Facilities. Clark Air Base, the only major U.S. tactical air force installation in Southeast Asia, is home base for a tactical fighter wing and a tactical airlift wing. It is also the air logistics hub for all U.S. forces in the Western Pacific with major aircraft maintenance facilities and large stockpiles of fuel, ammunition and other military consumables. The Crow Valley Weapons Range, a part of Clark Air Base, where live tactical training can be conducted in an instrumented setting, is the only such facility available west of California. Clark has the greatest capacity for handling airlift of personnel and materiel in the Western Pacific.[7] Clark is also a major north-south and east-west communications hub.

Subic Bay Naval Base Complex—Naval Air Station, Naval Station, Naval Ship Repair Facility, and Naval Communications Station—can support combat operations of several carrier battle groups and provide logistics backup (fuel, ordnance, repair parts, and other military consumables) for naval operations throughout the Indian and Western Pacific Oceans.[8]

Because of their favorable location, military forces based in the Philippines can support operations that contribute to the pursuit of military objectives in both Northeast and Southeast Asia, and in the Indian Ocean as shown in the following table.[9]

U.S. Military Benefits from the Philippine Facilities

Area Supported	Operation Supported
Southeast Asia	1. Offset Soviet military presence 2. Threaten Soviet lines of communication to Southeast Asia from Soviet Far East 3. Support ground warfare in defense of allies 4. Defend Southeast Asian sea and air routes
Northeast Asia	1. Defend Southeast Asian sea and air routes 2. Defend trans-Pacific sea and air routes 3. Threaten sea routes from Europe to the Soviet Far East 4. Rear base support of ground warfare in defense of U.S. allies
Persian Gulf	1. Defend Southeast Asian sea and air routes 2. Way station on the air route from the United States to Diego Garcia 3. Rear base support of combat operations in defense of Persian Gulf oil fields

Problems Affecting Utility of the Facilities

Despite the military advantages derived from the use of the facilities in the Philippines today, three problems potentially may detract from their continued utility: Filipino fears of being dragged into a superpower war or even the wrong local war in Southeast Asia—because of U.S. commitments of limited concern to the Philippines—that may result in denial of American use of the facilities for out-of-area combat operations, e.g. in the Persian Gulf; civil unrest within the Philippines that may eventually lead to the insecurity of U.S. facilities or to a decision by the Philippine government to terminate the bases agreement; and the extreme needs of the Philippine economy that could drive the Philippine government's asking price for continuing the bases agreement beyond 1991 so high the U.S. government will decide that it cannot afford it.

Although not an imminent probability, losing the use of the facilities in the Philippines through any of these potential difficulties would necessitate major redeployment of U.S. forces in East Asia. Contingency planning for such a redeployment is prudent, and some has been done.[10] The next section examines redeployment options that have been discussed in open sources. Despite some contrary views, U.S. strategists are unlikely to abandon the strategic principle of forward defense that has guided general purpose force planning for both East Asia and Europe since the late 1940s.[11] Therefore a guiding principle for the analysis that follows is that redeployment, as far as possible, should be to locations within the theater.

Alternatives to the Present Basing Arrangement

There is general agreement among analysts who have studied the question that the military functions now performed by the Philippine facilities could be continued from other sites.[12] These analysts also agree that the favorable environment and inexpensive work force available in the Philippines cannot be easily duplicated anywhere. They believe any replacement facilities will be less efficient and will probably have a range of other drawbacks when compared with the facilities in the Philippines. But assuming the availability of adequate funding and the cooperation of potential host countries, maintaining military effectiveness after redeployment from the Philippines is feasible.

In addition to the facilities in the Philippines, the United States operates naval bases at Yokosuka, Japan, and on the island of Guam, and maintains minor naval installations at Sasebo, Japan, on Okinawa, and in Korea. Major Air Force, Navy, or Marine Corps aviation facilities exist on Guam, Okinawa, some of the main Japanese islands, and in Korea. Excess capacity at these other U.S. facilities in the region could accommodate some redeployed forces in peacetime, but existing facilities would need to be expanded or supplemented by new facilities to provide wartime capability equivalent to the current basing system with the Philippine facilities available.[13] For efficiency, location of the new bases should provide coverage of somewhat the same area as the Philippine bases currently provide.

The following section first examines the capabilities and limitations of other bases in the region to absorb the forces now using the Philippine facilities. Then possible sites for new bases are evaluated. Three general, not mutually exclusive, options are examined:

- Option 1: Relocation to other U.S. facilities in the region.
- Option 2: Relocation to an expanded base structure in Micronesia
- Option 3: Relocation to new facilities on the South China Sea

Use of an Australian airfield and, possibly, Australian port facilities would be a part of any of these options. The options will be evaluated for political feasibility, operational effectiveness, and cost, which are the primary factors involved in site selection for a base.

Relocation to Other U.S. Facilities in the Region

Political Feasibility

Except for the use of the Australian facilities, U.S. forces are already in these places. Obtaining permission to move additional forces in should

U.S. Facilities in the Philippines 113

present only the kinds of political problems encountered whenever it is proposed to insert more people and equipment into an already crowded place.

However, moving forces into either Korea or Japan could create other problems for the United States. Once in place in Northeast Asia, these forces would probably be regarded by the Japanese and Korean governments as committed to that theater. The Japanese government has a virtual veto over which military combat operations are suitable for U.S. forces based in Japan. And Japanese policy prohibits introduction of nuclear weapons into that country. These problems are not insurmountable but would have to be overcome.

Prospects for obtaining use of Australian airfield and port facilities seem favorable, although permission should not be assumed. The U.S. Naval Communications Station at Exmouth, Australia, has sometimes been an object of political controversy because Australians associate it with command and control of U.S. strategic submarines. Although Australians are friendly to Americans and allied by the ANZUS treaty, an antinuclear strain runs through Australian politics as it does throughout the Southwest Pacific, and this might create problems during negotiations.[14]

Operational Effectiveness

Operational effectiveness of base sites considers support capabilities (operation facilities, maintenance, and supply capabilities for the ships and aircraft supported by the base) and geographic location.

SUPPORT CAPABILITIES (SHIPS) *Berthing.* The only U.S. Navy ship homeported at Subic Bay, a cruiser, could easily be reassigned to Yokosuka, Japan, where the rest of its battlegroup is based and that base could easily accommodate this single additional ship. Other U.S. Navy ships use Subic Bay naval base as transients. They could visit other ports in the region instead.[15]

Neither Guam nor Okinawa has room for aircraft carriers in protected harbors, and none of the other U.S. bases in the region has the efficient co-location of airfield and ship berthing available at Subic.

Ship Repair. Subic's ship repair capability was painstakingly built up at great expense during the Vietnam War and is regarded as one of its major attributes.[16] But there are other places where ship repair could take place, albeit at a greater cost. Primary reliance could revert to Japan, where ship repair was performed before Subic was built up for the Vietnam War. Japanese ship repair manpower is well qualified and ample to expand the capacity at Yokosuka or at Sasebo if that became necessary, but additional real estate for facilities expansion is limited. But Guam's ship repair manpower is not sufficient to support a large expansion without augmentation from elsewhere, possibly even from the Philippines. Although out of the area, Pearl Harbor, Hawaii, has significant unused ship repair capacity that could handle any overload at facilities farther west. Finally, more reliance could be placed on repair ships, which could go to their customers and are capable of performing almost every kind of repair available at one of the shore-based ship repair activities except drydocking.

Ship Supply. Subic Bay Naval Base has large stockpiles of fuels, ordnance, repair parts, and other military consumables that would have to be relocated to Guam, Yokosuka, or Pearl Harbor. As in the case of ship repair, more reliance on supply ships would be required.

SUPPORT CAPABILITIES (AIRCRAFT) *Aircraft Accommodations and Maintenance.* Relocating the tactical fighter wing and tactical airlift wing from Clark may initially cause some overloading at new sites. Considerable base expansion would probably be necessary to handle the greater demands on U.S. airpower anticipated in event of a conflict in the region.

Some reassignment of missions might be required. For example, the tactical fighter wing at Clark has air defense of the Philippines and Southeast Asian air space as its primary mission and a secondary mission in Northeast Asia. Moving the air wing to Guam, which has no fighters presently assigned, would remove it from the area of both its primary and secondary missions. Moving it to Japan or Korea would enhance its ability to meet its secondary mission, but its primary mission would become all but impossible. Air defense of Southeast Asian air space could, in either case, be reassigned to carrier wings. That would entail adjusting Pacific Theater carrier force level requirements.

Space could probably be found at Okinawa to relocate the tactical airlift wing, which serves the Western Pacific and Indian Ocean regions. Some additional airlift aircraft, perhaps with longer legs, would probably be needed to compensate for the less advantageous new location.

Aircraft Supply. As is the case with ship supply capability, some warehousing, fuel storage, and magazines sufficient for peacetime usage are available in the other U.S. bases in the region. But additional storage would be required to compensate for the loss of capacity of the Philippines facilities.

GEOGRAPHIC LOCATION Redeployment from the Philippines to other U.S. bases in the region would move our forces closer to their mission area in Northeast Asia and farther from Southeast Asia and the Persian Gulf. For a limited war in Northeast Asia, this redeployment would be more efficient. However, for other contingencies (including those requiring neutralization of Soviet bases in Vietnam), increased transit times from out-of-area bases to the Southeast Asian scene of operations could result in a requirement for more forces. Several other consequences, some adverse, could also result.

Most of the U.S. forces in the Western Pacific would be concentrated in Northeast Asia where they would be much closer to potentially hostile air and naval bases in the Soviet Union. While concentration has merit in warfighting, as a peacetime posture it unnecessarily subjects too many forces at one time to surprise attack.

Moving U.S. forces out of the South China Sea to bases in Okinawa, Guam and Japan leaves the Soviets and their well-armed Vietnamese clients in a position to dominate Southeast Asia in peacetime from their permanent, well-equipped bases while the United States could maintain an offsetting military presence only by underway patrols and visits to foreign ports.[17]

U.S. forces based in Northeast Asia are well located to interdict the Soviet lines of communication between their bases in Vietnam and the Soviet Far East, but could not cover Soviet lines of communication to Vietnam via the Indian Ocean.

Moving U.S. forces out of the Philippines would make the sea and air routes from the United States to the Indian Ocean via the Pacific seem less secure. U.S. defense planners might decide that the routes via Suez or the Cape of Good Hope were, on the whole, more reliable.

Current U.S. airlift aircraft need a stepping stone somewhere west of U.S. bases at Guam and Okinawa to enable them to reach their destinations in the Indian Ocean with militarily useful payloads.[18]

Cost Considerations

This section examines the cost of this option in three categories: military construction and other moving costs, the costs of new required forces, and operations and maintenance costs.

MILITARY CONSTRUCTION AND OTHER MOVING COSTS Moving to existing bases would minimize military construction and other moving costs. Many facilities similar to those in the Philippines are already in place. Although they would probably require expansion, this usually costs less than starting from scratch. All U.S. bases that would be candidates for receiving redeployed forces are in populated areas where real estate may be obtained only at a premium if available at all.

COST OF NEW FORCES As indicated in the section on geographic location, moving away from Southeast Asia could result in a requirement for more forces. The decrease in military effectiveness for today's naval and air forces operating 1,500–2,000 miles farther from base is in the neighborhood of 15–20 percent.[19] Applying that factor to the Pacific Fleet's Battle Force would result in a peacetime requirement for one or two more battle groups to perform tasks presently assigned to sea-based aviation in Southeast Asia. In wartime, since land-based fighter cover would no longer be available from the Philippines, the number of Navy battle groups would need to be increased even more to make up for that deficiency. Assuming one additional battle group on station between the Philippines and Vietnam would be sufficient (an arguable assumption even if the Soviets do not move into the Philippines), at least two more battle groups would need to be added because of the absence of land-based fighters. Thus three or four additional battle groups might be required in a war that involved substantial Southeast Asian combat operations, more if the Soviets should move into the Philippine bases. Other kinds of forces, (e.g. antisubmarine aircraft, airlift aircraft and their tankers, convoy escorts) would also require augmentation.

On the other hand, if the Philippines, under wartime pressures, made their bases available again to the United States these forces would not be required.

OPERATIONS AND MAINTENANCE COSTS Extra operating costs would be incurred from this move because of increased distance to Southeast Asian operating areas, because more port and terminal expenses would have to be paid when ships and aircraft made additional port calls than when they could use the Philippine facilities, and because wages in Japan, Korea, and Guam are higher than wages paid to Filipino base workers. If the ship repair facility at Guam were expanded, the Guamanian work force would have to be augmented by costly imported labor until more native workers could be trained.

Relocation to an Expanded Base Structure in Micronesia

Review of the preceding option will show that it suffers from two defects: there would not be enough capacity in the remaining bases in the region to support the increased forces and higher operating tempos needed for a war, and forces based in those places would be poorly positioned for operations in Southeast Asia. Southeast Asian sea and air routes are of great importance to the United States and of vital importance to our Asian friends and allies. Expanding the base structure in Micronesia could cure these defects to some extent. The U.S. government has examined the possibility of expanding the Naval and Air Force bases on Guam and reopening and modernizing some World War II facilities on Saipan, Tinian, and Palau to increase the overall capacity of the base structure and provide a nearer support facility for Southeast Asian operations than Guam.

Political Feasibility

Guam is an organized, unincorporated territory of the United States. Tinian and Saipan are part of the Northern Marianas Islands, a Commonwealth of the United States since 1976. Any political difficulty over the execution of this option in those places would be settled as a domestic issue. The United States government owns large tracts of land on Guam and has a fifty-year renewable lease on 18,000 acres of land in nearby Tinian, Saipan, and Farallon de Medinalle Islands, which includes the real estate proposed for base development. Domestic issues raised against base development include opportunity cost (money and land) and whether bases are acceptable neighbors. These issues can usually be resolved when the financial and other benefits to the community of having the bases are well enough publicized.

Palau is in transition from a United Nations Strategic Trust status to a new relationship with the United States as a "Freely Associated State." The Compact of Free Association with Palau, which was before the U.S. Congress for approval as of this writing, provides that the United States will have full authority and responsibility for security and defense matters in or relating to Palau. The Compact grants base rights to the United States, but with a provision that the United States will not use, test, store, or dispose of nuclear, toxic chemical, gas or biological weapons intended for use in warfare.

However, agreement further provides that the United States has the right to operate nuclear-capable or nuclear-propelled vessels and aircraft within the jurisdiction of Palau without either confirming or denying the presence or absence of nuclear weapons. Antinuclear activists in Palau oppose this latter provision and have continued to fight approval of the Compact at the polls and in the courts.

Operational Effectiveness

SUPPORT CAPABILITIES (SHIPS) *Berthing.* Palau's harbor could accommodate a carrier battle group, and there is an air strip that could be lengthened to accommodate high-performance aircraft. About 1,400 acres of ammunition storage are available in an area that has been reserved for the U.S. base by the Compact of Free Association. But almost everything else needed for a naval base would have to be built. Space is more limited than in the Philippines, and the manpower pool from which base workers could be drawn is also very limited.

The Naval Base at Guam has usable facilities, but the harbor would need extensive dredging to accommodate a carrier. Like Palau, Tinian has air fields but not many usable structures. Harbors on Tinian and Saipan are not well protected. They are barely large enough to support the airfields logistically.

Ship Repair. The Ship Repair Facility at Guam could be expanded, but skilled manpower would have to be imported until native workers could be trained.

Ship Supply. Guam's magazine and supply activities are small, and space is at a premium on Guam and Palau, but Tinian and Saipan have room for warehousing to be built.[20]

SUPPORT CAPABILITIES (AIRCRAFT) Anderson Air Force Base on Guam has a longer runway than Clark but is short of ramp space and passenger handling facilities, the essential requirements for the large-scale air-craft operations for which Clark has been configured.[21] An additional airfield on Guam, Northwest Guam Air Force Base, is closed and not maintained, and Tinian has a leftover World War II B-29 air base that could be reactivated and modernized into a major airlift staging base. Tinian's main deficiency is its inadequate port facility that even in World War II logistically limited its air operations.[22] The lease of the land on Tinian and Saipan includes the port facilities on both islands, but some planners worry that port facilities could not be made adequate to support modern high-tempo air operations.

Runways at Palau's two airfields are 7,000 and 7,600 feet long, extendable to about 10,000 feet, which would allow routine military airlift operations if parking space and passenger facilities were also provided.

GEOGRAPHIC LOCATION Building a significant base structure in Micronesia would cure some of the location problems found in analyzing option 1. U.S. peacetime posture would not have forces overly concentrated too near Soviet air and naval bases, and the addition of facilities in Palau would enable defense of the sea and air routes through Lombok, Sunda and Ombai–Wetar Straits, which handle much of the traffic of very large tankers from the Indian Ocean to Northeast Asia.[23]

But some of the most troublesome location problems would not be solved by this second option alone. The Soviets and their Vietnamese clients operating from their permanent bases could still have a peacetime advantage in the South China Sea over the United States, and the back door to their Vietnamese bases would remain open in wartime. Airlift aircraft would still be a requirement for additional U.S. forces because China Sea operations would still be at somewhat greater distance than from the Philippines. Air defense of the sea and air routes in the South China Sea would still have to be assigned to carrier battle groups.

Cost Considerations

This option would result in significantly higher military construction and other moving costs than simply moving into existing facilities as in option 1. In 1983, Admiral Robert Long, then Commander-in-Chief,

The Philippine Bases

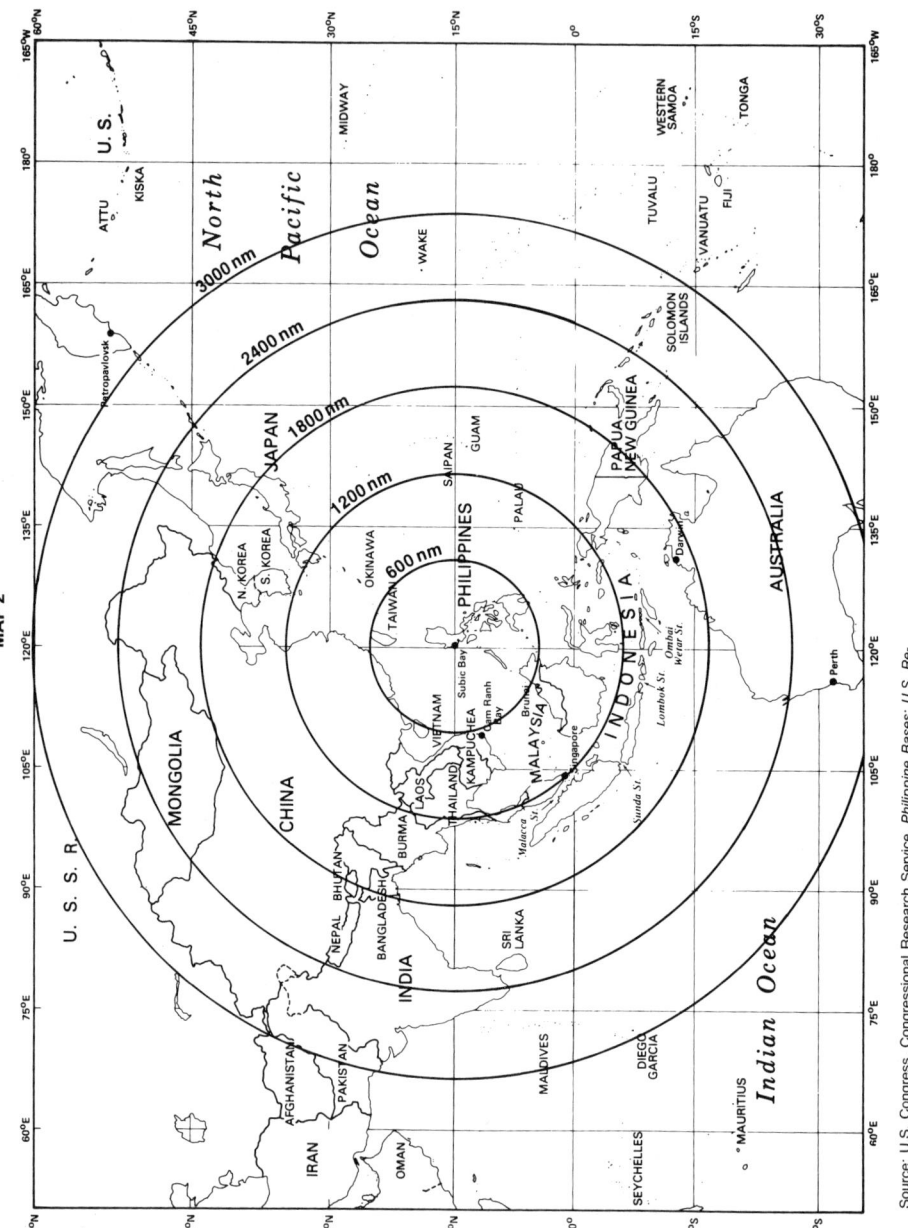

MAP 2

Source: U.S. Congress. Congressional Research Service. *Philippine Bases: U.S. Redeployment Options*, p. CRS 5. No. 86-44 F. February 20, 1986. The Library of Congress. Washington D.C. 1986.

U.S. Pacific Command, told the Congress such costs could be in the neighborhood of $3–$5 billion over five to six years.[24] Force procurement costs would be less than option 1 because forces operating from Palau would have a shorter transit time to their operating stations than from Guam or Japan. Operations and maintenance costs should be less also because fewer port calls would be made and shorter distances would be required.

Relocation to New Facilities on the South China Sea

New bases on the South China Sea would cure most of the problems remaining from option 2. Depending on the location and size of the new facilities, some of the base reactivation in Micronesia might be omitted. But political difficulties both at home and in potential host countries make it likely that new facilities would not be as capable as Clark Air Base and Subic Bay Naval Base. Therefore some of the elements of options 1 and 2 would need to be implemented. The "new" facilities on the South China Sea might have to be established under sharing arrangements with the new host country.

Political Feasibility

This option requires finding a new host country from a very short list: Indonesia, Thailand, Singapore, Malaysia, and Brunei.[25] Regional politics greatly influence the attitude of individual countries toward hosting U.S. bases on their territory. The U.S. presence in Southeast Asia has permitted these countries to avoid taking sides in the Sino–Soviet rivalry in East Asia. This fosters favorable attitudes toward an American base, as does concern over Vietnam's military strength, which most observers believe exceeds their purely defensive requirements. But all these countries are members of ASEAN, which seeks to remain independent of superpowers.

Indonesia is the country most likely ultimately to become the strongest regional actor if the great powers leave, and therefore has the least incentive to prolong U.S. military presence in the region. An island nation, Indonesia feels less threatened by land-bound Vietnam than do its neighbors on the mainland of Asia. The Indonesians are closer to the Soviets than to the Chinese. But in 1986, the Indonesian government was involved in a dispute with the government of India over Indian development of a military base on Great Nicobar Island, near the Indian Ocean end of Malacca Strait, because of rumors that Soviet use of the base is contemplated.[26] When approached by the Philippine foreign secretary in the fall of 1987 about their position on keeping the Americans in the Philippines, the Indonesians are reported to have declined to take a position. They are unlikely to agree to host a new American base on their territory.

Thailand hosted U.S. air bases until the U.S. withdrawal from Vietnam in 1975 left them exposed to take their neighbor's criticisms for backing a discredited foreign power. Since expelling the bases, they have sought to walk the tightrope between China and the Soviet client, Vietnam, with respect to the Kampuchean refugees in their border zones. But their history as a host for U.S. facilities in the past, the threat from Vietnam, and their closer relationship with the Chinese—who may find a nearby U.S. military presence useful in their dealings with Vietnam—may combine under the right circumstances to make Thailand a promising potential host country in the future.

The former British base at Singapore is remembered as one of Lord Fischer's "five keys that lock up the world." The naval dockyard has been turned over to commercial use. Until their Vietnamese base became available, the Soviets regularly used Singapore's maintenance facilities for their ships. The government of Singapore once offered to make base facilities available to the Americans but has not repeated the offer recently. Singapore's source of income is primarily as a business center for the region. It especially needs stability and would probably welcome an American presence, not only because of the Sino–Soviet rivalry but also because of latent regional rivalries that have been held in check by the American presence. Singapore is a good prospect to host a new American base or, at least, to accord U.S. ships and aircraft the same privileges formerly enjoyed by the Soviets.

Malaysia seems closer to Indonesia in their attitude toward the Sino–Soviet power struggle and whether the American presence is needed in the region. Although not as safe from the Vietnamese as Indonesia, Malaysia nevertheless probably feels less threatened than Thailand. When approached by the Philippine foreign secretary, it, also, declined to take a formal position on Philippine extension of the bases agreement, although Prime Minister Mahathir has publicly expressed a need for some countervailing presence so long as the Soviets are at Cam Ranh Bay. The official position of the Malaysian government has been to favor superpower withdrawal from Southeast Asia. It is not entirely clear whether that position would prevail if faced with the withdrawal of only one of the superpowers, but Malaysia is not regarded as a promising potential host for new U.S. facilities.

Until the Iran–Contra donnybrook in American politics during 1987, Brunei was the most favorably disposed of the Southeast Asian countries toward keeping the American presence in their region, but that has changed because of the embarrassment that came to their ruler over the disclosure in the American media of his help for the Nicaraguan contras. At this time there is little likelihood that Brunei would agree to host a new American base.

Even assuming success in finding a new host country, domestic opposition in the United States to extensive military construction in Southeast Asia might arise. Still smarting over having to leave fine bases for the Soviets to use in Vietnam, the U.S. public and the Congress may react to the necessity to move out of the Philippines by balking at proposals to build more new bases in yet other foreign countries. Still, the operational advantages of a position on the South China Sea are so great that this option should be considered despite a pessimistic evaluation of its political feasibility.

Operational Effectiveness

Because of the pessimistic outlook for base rights in Indonesia, Malaysia and Brunei, this section will examine possible sites only in Singapore and Thailand.

SUPPORT CAPABILITIES (SHIPS) All the countries considered in the preceding section have welcomed occasional port calls by U.S. ships. When accompanied by a repair ship and supply ships, a port call by other warships can be turned into a logistics visit. When the logistics ships are permitted to remain in port indefinitely and to contract for port services and supplies from local commercial sources, the port then has most of the attributes of a naval base.[27] But neutrality requirements limit the length and kinds of logistics activities permissible during a wartime port call. Policy considerations often have the same effect in peacetime. So a formal agreement covering both peacetime and wartime use of a harbor and its facilities is desirable.

Singapore's facilities and history as a naval base make it a desirable candidate for a new U.S. facility on the South China Sea. Choosing a Thai port would involve more facilities construction and, possibly, extensive dredging to make a shelter for an aircraft carrier. On balance, Singapore would be the better choice for ship operations.

SUPPORT CAPABILITIES (AIRCRAFT) Singapore's crowded airfield has very little excess capacity that could be set aside for a major airlift operation but could probably handle logistics flights for ship support and some antisubmarine operational flights. Singapore has no real estate upon which a new air facility could be built. In contrast, former U.S. air bases in Thailand functioned effectively during the Vietnam war and could do so again if made available to the United States.

GEOGRAPHICAL LOCATION Neither Singapore nor Thailand would be freely accessible from the east against Soviet opposition from their Vietnamese bases during wartime. But with a linking base on Palau, facilities in those countries could be sustained logistically and would complement the remainder of the Pacific basing structure. An airlift way stop in Australia, for safety and redundancy, would still be desirable if this option were chosen.

Cost Considerations

This option would permit a trade-off between base building expenses and the cost of some additional new forces. Military construction and moving costs of this option would be high, as they would be additive to most of those of option 2. But availability of the bases nearer the South China Sea would reduce force-level requirements. Operations and maintenance costs would be higher than if the Philippine facilities were still available.

Summary of Options

- Two kinds of deficiencies would need to be overcome to compensate for the loss of the facilities in the Philippines: the overall capacity of the Pacific base structure would be inadequate and the Soviet military presence in Southeast Asia would no longer be offset by a comparable U.S. military presence.
- None of the options examined in this analysis is satisfactory by itself, but a plan that combines elements of all three options could cure these deficiencies at affordable costs.
- Relocation of some aviation units to Japan and Korea, where the missions of the forces are compatible with such a relocation, could make more efficient use of the bases in those countries.
- Subic's ship repair capability could be replaced by increasing the ship repair capability in Japan and Guam.

- The capability of the base structure in Micronesia could be increased to compensate for the loss of the capacity of the facilities in the Philippines.
- An arrangement with a Southeast Asian country or countries for U.S. military use of port and airfield facilities on the South China Sea would facilitate, but is not essential to, U.S. military operations in that region.
- Facilities for an airlift waypoint in Australia would improve the utility of the Pacific air route from the U.S. mainland to the Indian Ocean.
- Use of port facilities on Australia's north or northwest coast would contribute to U.S. defense of the sea lanes through the Indonesian straits that run east of the Philippines, outside the South China Sea, should defense of that alternate route become necessary.

Alva M. Bowen, Jr., Captain USN, retired, served 30 years in the Navy and 12 years in the Foreign Affairs and National Defense Division of the Congressional Research Service. He is the author of Philippine Bases: U.S. Redeployment Options, 1986. *A veteran of many years of operational experience in the western Pacific, he has written on Naval Affairs and the Asia–Pacific and Indian Ocean regions for various professional journals.*

Notes

1. U.S. military presence in the Philippines is based on provisions of the 1946 *Treaty of General Relations Between the United States of America and the Republic of the Philippines* (61 Stat.1174 TIAS 1568) that granted independence to the Philippines but reserved the use of such bases as the two governments deemed necessary for their mutual defense. This provision was implemented in 1947 by an executive *Agreement Between the United States of America and the Republic of the Philippines Concerning Military Bases.* (61 Stat.4019. TIAS 1775.), amended from time to time. In addition to the bases agreement, a 1951 *Mutual Defense Treaty Between the United States of America and the Republic of the Philippines* (59 Stat. 1021. TIAS 2529.) and the *Southeast Asia Collective Defense Treaty* (59 Stat. 1031. TIAS 3170) (Manila Pact) further define the formal defense partnership between the two countries.
2. This amendment confirmed an earlier, unpublished agreement to the same effect. In 1959, U.S. Ambassador Charles E. Bohlen and the Philippine Secretary of Foreign Affairs, Felixberto M. Serrano, signed an agree-

ment that committed the United States government to consult with the government of the Philippines "prior to the operational use of the U.S. bases for military combat operations, other than those conducted in accordance with United States–Mutual Defense Treaty and Southeast Asian Collective Defense Treaty" or "the establishment by the United States of long range missiles (IRBM or ICBM) on United States bases in the Philippines". This agreement remained unpublished until a congressional committee published it during the Vietnam War. *U.S. Congress. Senate. Hearings: United States Security Agreements and Commitments Abroad.* September 30–October 20, 1969. 91st Congress, 1st Session, Washington, D.C. U.S. Govt. Print. Off. 1969. p. 24.
3. According to an amendment to the agreement dated September 1966. Thereafter the agreement is subject to termination by either side on one year's notice.
4. For a more detailed treatment of this theme see "Stability in the Pacific Basin" in U.S. Congress, Joint Economic Committee, *The U.S. Role in a Changing World Political Economy: Major Issues for the 96th Congress,* Joint Committee Print. June 25, 1979. 96th Congress, 1st Session, Washington, D.C.: Govt. Print. Off., 1979.
5. For a recent statement of this position see U.S. Department of Defense, *Annual Report to the Congress: Fiscal Year 1988,* January 12, 1987, p. 49.
6. The Soviets maintain a permanent force in Southeast Asia of about 30 ships, including submarines, and 8 Bear, 16 Badger and 14 MiG-23 aircraft. In time of tension, these forces could be augmented from Soviet Air Force and Pacific Fleet units based in the Soviet Far East that are more numerous than any Asian country except China could match, and more modern than any but the Japanese.
7. According to then Commander-in-Chief, Pacific Command, Admiral Robert Long, Clark Air Base is essential to the Pacific–Indian Ocean airlift system. U.S. Congress. House. Committee on Foreign Affairs. *United States–Philippine Relations and the New Base and Aid Agreement.* Hearings before the Subcommittee on Asian and Pacific Affairs. June 17, 23 and 28, 1983. 98th Congress, 1st Session, Washington, D.C. U.S. Govt. Print. Off. 1983. p. 8.
8. For a more detailed description of the U.S. facilities at Clark and Subic, see U.S. Congress. Congressional Research Service. *Philippine Bases: U.S. Redeployment Options.* Report No. 86–44. February 20. 1986. Library of Congress. Washington. 1986. Appendix 1 pp. 38–44.
9. This table is taken from Alva M. Bowen, Jr., "The Philippine–American Defense Partnership" in *Rebuilding a Nation: Philippine Challenges and American Foreign Policy.* Carl H. Lande, ed. (Washington, D.C.: The Washington Institute Press, 1987), p. 462.
10. In the spring of 1986, in response to a requirement by the Senate Appropriations Committee, the Secretary of Defense submitted a classified report to the Congress addressing potential redeployment sites and military

construction programming that might be necessary to prepare alternate facilities for the missions now accomplished by the Philippine bases.
11. For a contrary view of the need for the U.S. to continue maintaining a military presence in Southeast Asia, see Paul M. Kattenburg, "The case for Ending the Special Relationship and Leaving the U.S. Bases in the Philippines," in *Rebuilding a Nation: Philippine Challenges and American Diplomacy.* Carl H. Lande, ed., *op. cit.* p. 547.
12. The following unclassified reports were examined in connection with this study:

Cheri Lynn Connilogue. *New Bases for Old: An Unusual View of the Philippines Bases Problem.* M.A. Thesis. Naval Post Graduate School. Dec.1984. 91 p.

LCOL Terrence J. Connell et al. *Republic of the Philippines—A Strategic Study.* Carlyle Barracks, Penn. U.S. Army War College. June, 1977. 60 p.

Alvin J. Cottrell and Thomas J. Moorer. *U.S. Overseas Bases: Problems of Projecting Military Power Abroad.* Washington Papers. v. 5, No.47. Beverly Hills CA. Center for Strategic and International Studies/Sage Publications. 1977. 67 p.

Alvin J. Cottrell and Robert J. Hanks. *The Military Utility of the U.S. Facilities in the Philippines.* Significant Issues Series, v. 2, No. 11. Washington D.C. Center for Strategic and International Studies. 1980. 34 p.

Alvin J. Cottrell. "Key U.S. Bases in the Philippines." *National Defense* v. 67 Dec. 1982: 31, pp. 34–36.

Edmond Gannon. *Alternative Sites for U.S. Philippine Bases.* U.S. Library of Congress. Congressional Research Service. Washington, D.C. 1977. 70 p.

Lawrence E. Grinter. *The Philippine Bases: Continuing Utility in a Changing Strategic Context.* National Security Affairs Monograph Series, 80–2. Washington D.C. National Defense University. February 1980. 77 p.

LCOL Clifford R. Kreiger and Capt. Robert E. Webb. *The Strategic Importance of U.S. Military Facilities in the Philippines.* Carlyle Barracks, PA. U.S. Army War College. May 1983. 181 p.

13. The Pacific base structure has a "surge" capability to permit some level of contingency operations above routine peacetime schedules while expansion to full wartime capability takes place. An unexpected move from the Philippines could take advantage of this surge capability for a while, but prudence would require that the overall capacity of the base structure be adjusted as soon as possible to compensate for the loss of the capacity of the Philippine facilities.
14. For a more detailed treatment of the potential impact of antinuclear weapons sentiment on U.S. naval operations, see Alva M. Bowen and Ronald O. Rourke, "Ports for the Fleet" in *US Naval Institute Proceedings/Naval Review 1986.* May, 1986, Vol. 112/5/999. Naval Institute. Annapolis, MD. 1986 p. 147–151.
15. In peacetime, ship visits are an accepted norm. In wartime, neutrality requirements often restrict the duration and kinds of activities permissible during a warship visit to a foreign port.
16. In addition to expanded shops and new, advanced equipment to expand Subic's Ship Repair Facility, an intensive training program was conducted,

involving the importation of skilled technicians from Japan and the United States, to augment the small Filipino work force on hand in 1963. Today there is an ample, highly skilled ship repair force whose work costs less than any repair facility in the Pacific by a factor of 7 to 10.
17. Most naval analysts regard the South China Sea as the Asian equivalent of the Mediterranean. U.S. withdrawal from the South China Sea might thus be regarded as the strategic equivalent of pulling the Sixth Fleet out of the Mediterranean to the British Isles and the Azores. Under this option, the U.S. naval peacetime presence in the South China Sea would have to be maintained by scheduling port calls to foreign countries there on a regular basis. Some of these visits already take place, but their frequency and number would have to be dramatically increased to offset the adverse impression created by a U.S. withdrawal from the Philippines. "Port calls" refer to all kinds of visits, formal and informal, for reasons varying from showing the flag to emergency repairs or refuge from storm.
18. The 3,366 nautical mile Clark–Diego Garcia leg is the longest on the military airlift route to the Persian Gulf. Anderson Air Force Base on Guam is 1,423 n.m. farther east than Clark. To fly this extra distance nonstop and unrefueled would require a 60 percent payload reduction for a C-5A aircraft and no payload for a C-141B. With Clark not available, an alternate route via Guam and Darwin, Australia adds up to 2,400 n.m. to the trip but keeps the legs short enough to permit operationally useful payloads. Inflight refueling is possible but would require extra inflight tanker planes. Clifford R. Kreiger and Robert E. Webb. *The Strategic Importance of U.S. Military Facilities in the Philippines.* U.S. Army War College. Carlyle Barracks, PA. May 20, 1983.
19. This table shows how increasing distance from base to operating area increases force requirements because on-station time decreases as a percent of total cycle time.

Distance to Base-Op Area (n.m)	Roundtrip Transit, 15 Knots (Days)	On-station Days, 60-day cycle (Assumes 10 Days at Bases) (Days)	On-station Time as a Percentage of Total Cycle Time (%)	No. Carrier Battle Groups Required to Keep Two on Station
1,000	5.5	44.6	74	3
2,000	11.1	38.9	61	3
3,000	16.6	33.4	56	4
4,000	22.2	27.8	46	5
5,000	29.6	20.4	34	6

Such a table can be prepared for any kind of force or mission. Overall force requirements are aggregates of many such tables. This table was adapted from a similar table presented by Desmond P. Wilson Jr. in U.S. Congress. Senate and House. Joint Senate–House Armed Services Subcommittee. *Hearings on CVN 70 Aircraft Carrier.* 91st Congress, 2d Session. Washington, D.C. Govt. Print. Off. 1970 p. 574.

20. About one-third of Guam's total area is owned by U.S. military, and this has become a sore point with the local populace, who would rather use their own territory for their burgeoning tourist trade. Despite the large proportion of land dedicated to military use, Guam's warehouse and magazine capacity are so limited that a plan to homeport a U.S. destroyer squadron there was dropped in the early 1970s. Clifford R. Kreiger and Robert E. Webb *op. cit.* p. 124–125.
21. Clark Air Base can park 12 C-5A, 17 C141B or 118 C130 airlift aircraft while Anderson AFB and Agana Naval Air Station on Guam can only park 5 C-5A, 19 C-141B or 34 C-130 between them. See Clifford R. Kreiger and Robert E. Webb, *op. cit.* p. 121.
22. *Ibid.*, p. 123.
23. The shorter route via the Malacca Strait is too shallow and too crowded for these very large ships. The alternate route adds about 1,400 n.m. (three days) to the trip. Use of Australian port facilities could supplement Palau's for this task.
24. U.S. Congress. House. Committee on Foreign Affairs. *United States–Philippines Relations and the New Base and Aid Agreement. op cit.*
25. To be complete, the People's Republic of China and Taiwan should be added to the list, but political problems associated with negotiating base rights from either eliminate them from consideration at the outset.
26. "India and Indonesia in dispute over Malacca Strait Base", *Jane's Defense Weekly,* October 4, 1986.
27. Since its beginnings in 1946, the U.S. Sixth Fleet has used Naples, Italy, in this fashion. An important key to modern fleet support is a nearby airfield capable of receiving logistics flights and suitable staging facilities to receive, store and transfer the materials. Ships can perform this staging function if the airfield is not too inconveniently located with respect to the port.

The Military Bases and Postwar U.S.–Philippine Relations

William E. Berry, Jr.

On Subic Naval Base in the Philippines, there is a street corner where Burgos Street intersects Dewey Avenue. Burgos Street is named after Father Jose Burgos, one of the most famous martyrs of the Philippine revolution against Spain. He and two other priests were executed in 1872, allegedly as a result of their participation in anti-Spanish activities. They became symbols of Philippine nationalism and resistance to external control. Admiral George Dewey was the hero of the battle of Manila Bay and an early supporter of the continuation of American political, economic, and military involvement in the Philippines.

For the student of Philippine–American relations, this intersection is particularly symbolic because in the postwar era, American security interests frequently have conflicted with Philippine nationalism. There are few issues that better illustrate this conflict between the two countries than the retention of the military bases. The questions over the 1947 Military Bases Agreement (MBA) and the subsequent amendments to it have focused the debate in the past and continue to do so with the approach of completion of the MBA's fixed term in 1991. The manner in which American and Filipino negotiators attempt to resolve these differences will have a direct effect upon U.S. security interests in Asia as well as Philippine–American relations. This brief history of the base negotiations since the end of World War II will seek to identify specific issues central to the forthcoming negotiations.

The views expressed in this paper are those of the author and not necessarily of the United States Air Force or Department of Defense.

The Philippines lay destitute at the end of the war. What was not destroyed during the Japanese occupation was destroyed during the liberation. No other country in Southeast Asia suffered the property damage the Philippines did. President Franklin Roosevelt promised on several occasions during the war that the United States would provide assistance to the Philippines after the Japanese were driven out, so it was only natural that the Philippine political leaders and people looked to the U.S. for comprehensive assistance programs. Three of the most immediate requirements were for rehabilitation assistance, a fair and equitable trade relationship, and a security guarantee.

The Philippine Trade Act was passed by both houses of the Congress and signed by President Truman in April 1946.[1] This legislation provided for free trade between the two countries for eight years until 1954, and then a graduated tariff would go into effect until full tariff duties would be reached in 1974. Quotas were established on several Philippine exports, and if these quotas were exceeded, full duty would be charged on the excess. The Philippine peso was pegged to the U.S. dollar, which meant that the Philippines could not devalue or revalue its currency without the approval of the president of the United States.

The free trade, quotas, and currency provisions were controversial in the Philippines, but the most onerous of the Trade Act provisions was what became known as the "parity clause." Section 341 stipulated that U.S. citizens would have the same rights as Filipinos to exploit and develop agricultural, timber, and mineral lands and to operate public utilities. In order for this provision to be implemented, the 1935 Philippine Constitution had to be amended because it required the development of Philippine natural resources be accomplished by the citizens of the Philippines or by corporations in which Filipinos owned at least 60 percent of the capital. Although these provisions of the Trade Act were unpopular with many Filipinos, economic necessities forced acceptance because access to the American market was critical for Philippine exports and capital goods had to be imported.[2]

Rehabilitation legislation was introduced and debated in the U.S. Congress at the same time as the trade bill. As a matter of fact, the Rehabilitation Act was also passed and signed by President Truman in April 1946.[3] This legislation provided for $620 million in vitally needed assistance and served as an important stimulus for Philippine recovery. However, one provision of the Rehabilitation Act negated many of the benefits and adversely affected Philippine public opinion at the time.

Section 601 required that the "parity clause" of the Trade Act be accepted and the constitution amended before rehabilitation funds would be released. Most Filipinos believed that the United States had a definite responsibility to provide assistance because of President Roosevelt's pledge during the war, but more important, because the Philippines remained a loyal ally during the Japanese occupation and suffered much loss of life and destruction as a result. To tie economic assistance programs to a constitutional amendment that would abridge Filipino rights and national sovereignty was highly unpopular.

Nonetheless, the Philippine Congress did amend the constitution as required in September 1946, and a national plebiscite ratified this amendment in March 1947 by a considerable margin.[4] Through these legislative actions in both countries, the Philippines received the rehabilitation assistance so desperately needed as well as trade preferences in the American market. But in the process, it became clear that these gains had to be balanced against definite restrictions on Philippine sovereignty. These Philippine concerns over the loss of sovereignty would be exacerbated by the negotiations on security issues.

During 1946 and 1947, the two countries held talks on security matters. These exchanges concerned the possible location of American military bases in the Philippines and the assignment of Army and Navy personnel to them. There is evidence to suggest that by October 1946 the United States, especially the U.S. military, began to downgrade the importance of retaining military bases in the Philippines. In a message to the U.S. Ambassador in Manila from Acting Secretary of State Dean Acheson, the Secretary advised that the Navy and War Departments had decided only to retain "minimum essential" supply garrisons in the Philippines, with the exact number of personnel involved to be agreed upon during the negotiations.[5]

In November, the Navy announced plans to abandon its bases in the Samar–Leyte area. The primary reason given publicly was their location in the Philippine typhoon belt, where they had been constructed for temporary use during the war. To replace or reinforce these bases would cost more money than the Navy was willing to spend.[6] Unofficially, a Navy spokesman indicated that there was concern the Congress would not appropriate the necessary funds to retain all of the bases in the Philippines and still build the facilities that the Navy wanted on Okinawa and Guam. According to this account, the naval leaders believed that bases on these smaller islands would be easier to protect since their defenses could be concentrated.[7]

One of the most important factors altering the American position on the bases was the opinion expressed by General Dwight Eisenhower, who at that time was Army Chief of Staff. In a letter from Secretary of War Robert Patterson to Secretary of State James Byrnes in late November 1946, Patterson advised that Eisenhower recommended all U.S. Army forces be withdrawn from the Philippines unless the Philippine government or the State Department desired that a small force be retained.[8] Eisenhower's position stemmed from his belief that future good relations between the United States and the Philippines were more important than the strategic value of U.S. bases.

Eisenhower's opinion carried considerable weight, not only because of his position in the Army and reputation, but also because he had spent several years in the Philippines on Douglas MacArthur's staff before the war. Patterson concurred with Eisenhower's recommendation, but primarily because of economic factors. He did not believe the U.S. Congress would appropriate the necessary funds based on the military's demands for facilities in Korea, Australia, Italy, Japan, and Germany. The Secretary of War also indicated that Admiral Chester Nimitz, Chief of Naval Operations, had informed him that the Navy bases in the Philippines had been reduced to such an extent that Army units were unnecessary to defend them.[9]

Byrnes agreed with the position taken by the War Department, save that a small force be retained for a short period if the Philippine government so requested, but on the understanding that it would eventually be withdrawn.[10] On December 4, 1946, Acting Secretary of State Acheson met with President Truman at the direction of the Secretaries of State, War, and Navy and obtained Truman's approval for the plan to withdraw all U.S. Army forces from the Philippines. Ambassador McNutt was then instructed to advise Philippine authorities that the United States was planning to reduce its forces in the islands.[11]

The Philippine perspective on the retention of the U.S. military presence was considerably different. In May 1946, Manuel Roxas, the last president of the Philippine Commonwealth and first president of the Republic of the Philippines after independence on July 4, 1946, came to Washington. In public comments, he indicated his support for the retention of the U.S. bases as the Philippine contribution to the maintenance of security in the Western Pacific.[12] Beyond this rationale for retention, there were two other benefits that Roxas perceived to be gained from continuing the security relationship with the U.S. First, Philippine security would be protected. Although there was little external threat in the immediate postwar period, the tremendous loss of life and property suffered during the war was a constant reminder of what could happen if aggression occurred. The Philippines did not have resources available to provide for its own defense, so the United States was the best alternative available. Second, the retention of the bases was a means to focus American concern and interest on the Philippines. Roxas understood that the United States had assumed a far more dominant international position after the war, with much of its attention focused on European recovery. He hoped that the continued base presence in his country would cause U.S. political and military leaders to give attention to Asia in general and the Philippines in particular as the new geopolitical forces worked their way in the postwar world.

In July 1945 the Commonwealth legislature passed Joint Resolution No. 4 that authorized the Philippine president to enter into negotiations with the United States on security issues.[13] Initial negotiations began under the leadership of President Sergio Osmena in 1945, but little was accomplished until after the presidential election in April 1946 and the granting of Philippine independence the following July.[14] In his early discussions with Ambassador McNutt, Roxas became aware of the sentiment of some influential Americans who believed the U.S. should reduce, or perhaps eliminate, its military presence. Obviously, Roxas was concerned about this because of the importance he attributed to the bases for Philippine security and the continuation of the bilateral relationship. He referenced Joint Resolution No. 4 and indicated this document was a "mandate and settled policy of the Philippine people."[15] He also pointed to the many statements he had made confirming his belief that the bases should remain. After extensive discussions between the State and War Departments and the agreement of President Truman, the U.S. decided to retain a reduced force in the Philippines, but the majority of the soldiers and sailors would be withdrawn.[16]

As the negotiations progressed in the second half of 1946 and early 1947, the participants identified several difficult issues that took time and effort to resolve. Among the most difficult of these, and one that serves as a good example of how American security interests conflicted with Philippine nationalism, was criminal jurisdiction. It is almost inevitable that problems will arise between countries when the military forces of one of these are stationed in the territory of the other. Under these circumstances, a partial transfer of sovereignty is involved because two different legal systems are functioning within the same territory. The potential for problems is increased when one of the involved countries is the former colony of the other. To reduce the likelihood of conflict between the two legal systems, it is necessary to reach an accommodation and formalize this agreement in a written document between the sending and receiving states. This document stipulates which legal system has jurisdiction over what offenses. The MBA was designed in part to accomplish this function.

The U.S. Army and Navy wanted to retain the right to exercise exclusive jurisdiction over Americans, both military and civilians, assigned in the Philippines in order to maintain good order and discipline. This type of jurisdiction pertained during the colonial and Commonwealth periods and allowed the U.S. to exercise jurisdiction over Americans regardless of where an offense occurred. For Roxas and other Filipinos, this amounted to extraterritoriality and went against the Philippine judicial system, which, in turn, was based on the American model.[17] They sought instead concurrent jurisdiction, in which jurisdiction is shared, based on where an offense occurred.

President Roxas was placed very much on the defensive because of this dispute over the highly emotional issue of criminal jurisdiction. He was in a particularly difficult position because the Trade Act and Rehabilitation Act were being debated at the same time as the MBA, all of which were controversial. In September 1946 he announced that he intended to consider any bases accord as a treaty that would require him to submit such an agreement to the Philippine Senate for ratification.[18]

It is interesting to speculate about Roxas' motivations for deciding to submit the bases agreement to the Senate. There were no requirements to do so in Joint Resolution No. 4 that authorized his negotiations on the bases. The most logical explanation is that Roxas was attempting to protect himself politically. He had taken the lead in supporting the "parity clause" and the constitutional amendment, both of which were unpopular with many Filipinos. For Roxas to have placed himself in the position of being responsible for the bases agreement, also unpopular with some of the same groups, would have given his political opponents another major issue to use against him in future political contests. By submitting the agreement to the Senate, he was able to share responsibility. This procedure also permitted Roxas and his chief negotiators to argue that they could not guarantee ratification if the United States continued to exert pressure on some of the very controversial issues, such as criminal jurisdiction.

Despite these efforts on the part of Roxas and his associates, the United States was in a far superior negotiating position than was the Philippines. The historical relationship between the two countries partly explains this advantage, but more important were the actual political and economic influences of the time. In reality, the Philippines needed the United States much more than the reverse. The evidence available in the cables between American political officials and Ambassador McNutt does not suggest that the U.S. used the threat of troop withdrawals as a negotiating ploy to force the Philippines to accept American demands. The U.S. position on force levels was determined primarily by economic and strategic considerations. The rapid and extensive demobilization of U.S. forces, coupled with increased tensions in Europe, dictated that the number of military personnel in the Philippines be reduced significantly. The stringent fiscal policies of the Truman administration also were important factors in reducing these forces. From the strategic perspective, there were other locations such as Guam and Okinawa that were more attractive to the military than the facilities in the Philippines. For all these reasons, the United States continued to take a hardline position in the negotiations and was successful in reaching an agreement very favorable to its interests.

The Military Bases Agreement

The Military Bases Agreement, signed on March 17, 1947, is a comprehensive document including twenty-nine separate articles.[19] Article I delimited the specific bases that were to be made available to the U.S. under a cost-free arrangement. There were two categories of such bases. One category included those bases that the U.S. was permitted to retain, while the second category listed additional facilities that the Philippines would make available on request. Sixteen bases were placed in the first category, Clark Air Base and Subic Naval Base among them, and seven were identified in the second category.

Space constraints do not permit a detailed review of all the specific MBA provisions.[20] Article XIII on criminal jurisdiction is instructive in understanding how the United States was able to protect and enhance its negotiating positions in this agreement. The MBA granted the U.S. the right to exercise exclusive jurisdiction over every individual, including Filipinos, who committed a crime on any base unless both the victim and accused were Philippine nationals, in which case the Philippines would exercise jurisdiction. Furthermore, if a Filipino was the victim of a crime that occurred on base and the perpetrator was an American, the U.S. would have jurisdiction. *Inter se* offenses, those involving only Americans off the bases, also were to be under U.S. jurisdiction.

It is clear from this brief review that the United States was granted exclusive jurisdiction rather than the concurrent jurisdiction the Philippines sought. In Philippine eyes, the fact that the U.S. could prosecute Philippine citizens who allegedly committed crimes on American military bases undercut the nation's sovereignty and demonstrated the extent to which many of the MBA provisions favored the U.S. The agreement was to remain in effect for 99 years from the time of acceptance, which referred to the date the MBA was ratified by the Philippine Senate. President Roxas submitted the MBA to the Senate on March 17, and the Senators ratified it on March 27, 1947 by a vote of 18–0 with three Senators absent.[21]

Despite this overwhelming ratification of the MBA, many ardent Philippine nationalists such as Senators Claro Recto and Tomas Confessor argued that the Philippines could never be truly independent as long as foreign military forces were stationed in the country and a form of extraterritoriality obtained. Further, they were not certain the United States would come to the assistance of the Philippines if the latter was attacked, and conversely, they feared that their country might be drawn into a war because of its security relationship with the U.S.[22] Because of these perceived deficiencies, they argued that the MBA be renegotiated. Philippine nationalism, particularly as influenced by the perception of attenuated sovereignty, conflicted with U.S. national security interests as evidenced in the retention of the bases. This tension between Philippine nationalism and U.S. security interests continues to the present.

Philippine demands for renegotiation increased as the specifics of the NATO and Japanese Status of Forces Agreements (SOFAs) became known in the early 1950s. In both of these agreements, the U.S. made significant concessions much more favorable to the host countries than in the MBA.[23] Criminal jurisdiction again provides a good comparison in support of the Philippine complaint. In both the NATO and Japanese cases, the United States granted a system of concurrent jurisdiction in which the signatory countries agreed to give "sympathetic consideration" to the requests of the other if that country had a particular reason for wanting to exercise jurisdiction over a certain offense. This procedure contrasted appreciably with the exclusive jurisdiction provided for in the MBA. Even more significant, the United States did not have the authority to prosecute local nationals in the NATO and Japanese SOFAs as it did in the MBA. Filipinos found it especially offensive that the U.S. was willing to grant more favorable rights and protections to Japan, the former enemy, than it was to the Philippines, its former colony and current ally.

In addition to the Philippine protestations that the MBA should be amended, the international situation in Asia had changed by the early 1950s, which actually improved the Philippine negotiating position. Mao's victory in China in late 1949 and the subsequent Chinese security treaty with the Soviet Union convinced the Truman administration that the containment strategy should be extended to Asia. In a famous January 1950 speech to the National Press Club, Secretary of State Acheson described a defensive perimeter running from the Aleutian Islands in the north through Japan and the Ryukyu Islands to the Philippines in the south and indicated that the United States was determined to protect and defend this perimeter.[24] Therefore, the Philippine installations became more important to the U.S. as forward bases to support the containment of the Soviet Union and China in Asia. In the attempt to assuage those in the Philippines, such as Senators Recto and Confessor, who expressed concern over the American commitment as an ally, the U.S. and the Philippines entered into a Mutual Defense Treaty signed in Washington in August 1951 just before the conclusion of the Japanese peace treaty in San Francisco.[25]

Negotiations to Revise the MBA

Both the Philippine demands for renegotiation and the changing international situation in Asia were factors in the decision to enter into talks in 1954. Vice President Carlos Garcia and Ambassador Raymond Spruance were the primary negotiators. The most important issues addressed were Philippine sovereignty over the bases, expansion of certain of the facilities, and clarification of some of the criminal jurisdiction provisions.[26] A major problem developed early in the negotiations when Attorney General Herbert Brownell issued an opinion that the titles to the bases occupied by the United States before Philippine independence still legally belonged to the U.S. even though sovereignty over these lands was transferred to the Philippines in July 1946.[27] President Ramon Magsaysay became so angered over this decision that he suspended the Garcia–Spruance negotiations before they were able to address the substantive issues.

In 1956, Vice President Richard Nixon traveled to Manila to participate in the tenth anniversary of Philippine independence. He held discussions with President Magsaysay, and at the conclusion of this visit, they issued a joint statement that indicated that the two leaders agreed to resume negotiations on the bases.[28] Further, Nixon stated that the U.S. would transfer all base titles to the Philippines, thereby refuting the Brownell opinion and reaffirming Philippine sovereignty over the bases. The Nixon visit cleared the way for renewal of the suspended negotiations.

The negotiations resumed in 1956, with Senator Emmanuel Pelaez the chief negotiator on the Philippine panel and former Undersecretary of the Army Karl Bendetsen in a similar position for the U.S. It soon became apparent that the respective panels were pursuing different objectives. The Americans were interested in modernizing and expanding the bases, while the Filipinos wanted to revise the MBA to ensure increased expressions of Philippine sovereignty.[29] Bendetsen stressed the security aspects of Philippine–American relations, especially the perceived threat from China, implying that the bases provided for Philippine security against this threat. Pelaez was less concerned about security but more concerned about criminal jurisdiction. He pointed out that in the ten years since independence, over 20 Filipinos had been killed by security guards while scavenging for shells and casings on U.S. bombing ranges, and he drew attention to the NATO and Japanese SOFAs to indicate these agreements respected host-country sovereignty much more than did the MBA.[30]

The composition of the two panels also provided further indications of the different objectives. The American delegation was composed almost entirely of military men whose main interests involved expanding the base facilities. On the other side, President Magsaysay appointed primarily members of the Congress to the Philippine panel. They wanted to revise the MBA and concentrated on the criminal jurisdiction article. Their argument was that all offenses committed on the bases that violated Philippine law, with the exception of those occurring during the performance of official duty, should be included under Philippine jurisdiction.[31] Obviously, this represented a major change to the MBA, and Bendetsen responded that the U.S. did not grant such jurisdiction to any country in which it had bases. To do so in the Philippine case would not only set an undesirable precedent, but also would adversely affect the morale of those assigned to the bases.[32]

The differences of opinion and perspectives evident in the Bendetsen–Pelaez negotiations clearly indicated a fundamental conflict between Philippine desires to protect and expand Philippine sovereignty over the bases and American efforts to guarantee that no concessions were made that would reduce the operational effectiveness of the bases and personnel assigned to them. This difference of opinion between the exercise of Philippine sovereignty and U.S. operational control over the bases was not resolved in the 1956 negotiations that ended inconclusively in December of that year, and remains a critical issue to the present.

By the end of the 1950s, certain changes were evident within the Philippines that directly influenced the base negotiations. Philippine nationalism was becoming much more of a dynamic force in Philippine–American relations. The "special relationship" that, in previous periods, was looked upon positively by most Filipinos was now being questioned by many, especially by political leaders who wanted to formulate Philippine foreign policy as an Asian country and not necessarily as a subordinate of the United States. As the bilateral relationship matured, it was inevitable that base negotiations would be on the center stage.

President Eisenhower appointed Charles Bohlen, a career diplomat, as U.S. Ambassador in early 1958. He began a series of negotiations with Secretary of Foreign Affairs Felixberto Serrano that would continue off and on for the better part of the next two years. Contrary to the Garcia–Spruance and Bendetsen–Pelaez negotiations, the talks between Bohlen and Serrano were held in private, out of the glare of daily newspaper accounts. Another factor that contributed to the success of these negotiations was the lack of a deadline.[33]

The first agreement reached established a Mutual Defense Board and provided for the assignment of a Philippine Liaison Officer to each of the military bases.[34] The Mutual Defense Board was to be composed of high-ranking Philippine and American military officers who would meet on a monthly basis or more frequently if required. Its purpose was to resolve problems that developed between the two countries about military matters. Specifically, the Board was to discuss those issues that arose under the MBA and provide for the necessary cooperation and consultation on other matters of mutual interest. The Liaison Officer was to be the primary advisor to the Base Commander on the observance of Philippine laws. He also was to advise the commander on problems involving Philippine nationals working on the bases and to serve as the point of contact between base officials and host country authorities.

Preliminary negotiations on other substantive issues began in October 1958. Bohlen and Serrano agreed on an agenda that identified four main topics of discussion. These topics were base operating procedures, land delimitation, military consultation and cooperation, and criminal jurisdiction.[35] They were able to reach an agreement on some of these topics during the course of the next year.[36] This agreement contained three sections that addressed consultations, the duration of the MBA, and mutual defense. The United States agreed to prior consultation with the Philippines on the operational use of the bases for all military combat actions that would be conducted, except those "in accordance with the United States Mutual Defense Treaty and the Southeast Asia Collective Defense Treaty." It was also agreed that no long-range missiles would be introduced into the Philippines without prior consultation.

Bohlen and Serrano reduced the length of the MBA from the original 99 years to 25. However, this new period would not go into effect until all the agreed formal documents were signed. This did not occur until the exchange of notes between Secretary of State Dean Rusk and Secretary of Foreign Affairs Narciso Ramos on September 16, 1966. Therefore the MBA's fixed term went to 1991,[37] after which it could be abrogated by either party, with one year's notice. To terminate earlier than 1991 required the concurrence of both parties, as in the original MBA article. The final agreement between Bohlen and Serrano, concluded just before Bohlen completed his assignment in December 1959, returned the city of Olongapo to Philippine jurisdiction.[38] From 1920 until this agreement, with the exception of the war years, the U.S. Navy had exercised control over this city of 65,000 adjacent to Subic Naval Base. This arrangement had been a source of friction for many years, and its return to Philippine jurisdiction reduced disputes between the Navy and local authorities.

On criminal jurisdiction, Serrano argued, as had Pelaez before him, that the MBA had to be brought into line with the NATO and Japanese agreements, particularly in rescinding U.S. authority to exercise jurisdiction over Filipinos on the bases. Bohlen took the position that the United States would not make a unilateral concession resulting in the reduction of U.S. jurisdiction.[39] They were unable to resolve this difference before Bohlen left the Philippines.

The next round of negotiations occurred in 1965, primarily as a result of Philippine demands that the criminal jurisdiction provisions be amended. President Diosdado Macapagal appointed Secretary of Justice Salvador Marino to conduct an investigation into a series of incidents that had occurred on the bases with Filipinos as the victims. Marino released his report in January 1965 that was critical of the manner in which American authorities handled these cases.[40] Senator Arturo Tolentino applied more pressure on Macapagal not only by referring to the Marino Report but also by making the point that the MBA was an affront to the Philippines because it implied the Philippine court system was incapable of meting out justice even to its own citizens since the U.S. had jurisdiction over Filipinos on the bases.[41] Once again, the military bases became embroiled in Philippine domestic politics.

In February 1965, Ambassador William McCormack Blair announced that the U.S. was prepared to make concessions to the Philippines on criminal jurisdiction.[42] Between February and August, Blair negotiated with Secretary of Foreign Affairs Mauro Menez, and they signed an amendment to the MBA on August 10, 1965.[43] In essence, this amendment met the Philippine demand that the MBA be brought in line with the NATO and Japanese SOFAs in that a system of concurrent jurisdiction was implemented. Each side promised to give "sympathetic consideration" to the requests of the other to waive the right to exercise jurisdiction in those cases of particular national interest. Certainly one of the most important changes from the Philippine perspective was contained in paragraph 4. The United States no longer had jurisdiction over Filipinos who committed crimes on military bases. In an attached Agreed Official Minute, the two countries established a Criminal Jurisdictional Implementation Committee (CJIC).[44] Representatives from both countries would serve on this committee and consult over matters relating to criminal jurisdiction that occurred from time to time.

Negotiations with the Marcos Regime

There were few serious efforts to renegotiate base issues during the late 1960s and early 1970s. However, the international situation affecting American–Philippine relations changed dramatically in the spring of 1975 with the communist victories in Vietnam, Cambodia, and Laos. U.S. commitments to its treaties and other obligations were called into question since the United States had been unable to prevent the defeats of its client states. President Ferdinand Marcos wasted little time in raising his concern over the Mutual Defense Treaty (MDT) and the military bases. He supported the continuation of the American presence in the region but questioned whether the U.S. would remain an Asian power because of congressional and public disillusionment with the Indochina experience.[45] Marcos also believed that he might be able to force the United States to increase its economic and military assistance programs through negotiations. He needed these increases because the insurgencies led by the Moro National Liberation Front and the New People's Army were becoming more serious. As an astute politician, Marcos was aware that base negotiations would allow him to wrap himself in the flag of Philippine nationalism at a time when his martial law regime was coming under increasing domestic criticism.

President Gerald Ford and Secretary of State Henry Kissinger tried to assuage Marcos' concerns. After a brief visit to the Philippines in December 1975, Ford and Marcos issued a joint communique.[46] They confirmed the importance of the MDT to the security of both countries and stressed that the bases should remain. It was agreed that additional negotiations should be conducted "in the clear recognition of Philippine sovereignty" and that these negotiations should begin as soon as practicable. Kissinger went even further in a speech in July 1976 when he stated that the American willingness to enter into talks with the Philippines to retain the bases was a strong indication of U.S. resolve to remain a regional military power.[47]

It is clear from the statements made by Marcos, Ford, and Kissinger that the military bases were taking on increased importance in addition to their military functions. For Marcos, negotiations on the bases were a means of increasing American economic and military assistance programs so that the Philippines could better contain the two insurgencies that were becoming much more of a threat. For Ford and Kissinger, the negotiations were a means to indicate the United States would remain an Asian power and meet its treaty commitments. The impending negotiations, therefore, had political and economic ramifications as well as military importance for the countries involved.

Additional Negotiations

Kissinger and Minister of Foreign Affairs Carlos Romulo began the talks in April 1976. Subsequently, Ambassador William Sullivan and Philippine Ambassador Eduardo Romualdez conducted most of the discussions. They established five working groups to study facilities, command and control, legal issues, labor problems, and taxation.[48] The Philippine negotiators presented 25 issues that they said needed to be resolved.[49] A few of these were relatively minor, such as whether the agreement should be authentic in both the Filipino and English language versions, but the majority were substantive in nature. Three of the most important were command and control procedures at the bases, nuclear weapons storage, and criminal jurisdiction.

The differences over command and control procedures reflected the basic dilemma that continued throughout the negotiations and still have not been settled, namely how to balance Philippine demands for increased sovereignty over the bases with U.S. insistence for unhampered military control. Of particular significance in the 1976 discussions was the Philippine position that, when national security was at stake, the Philippines should assume control over the operations and administration of the bases. The U.S. panel argued that such extended Philippine powers would violate the principle of unhampered military control.[50]

The question of nuclear weapons storage has been contentious since the immediate postwar period when Roxas and others argued that the U.S. bases should not be located in metropolitan areas because of the fear that they would become "magnets for attack" in case of a war. During the 1976 negotiations, the question was defined as follows:

"Whether the Philippines should allow the passage through Philippine airspace or waters, aircraft, vessels, or submarines carrying nuclear weapons or components thereof, or other unconventional weapons."[51] The Philippine negotiators argued that their country should not allow the introduction or storage of nuclear weapons, as these arms were clearly offensive and would impede efforts to improve relations with neighboring countries. The American counter to this argument was that U.S. global strategic effectiveness depended on not revealing where nuclear weapons were or were not stored, and that this was the policy employed with all allies.[52] The debate over criminal jurisdiction involved demands that the Philippines exercise increased jurisdiction over official duty and *inter se* cases. The American negotiators replied that the 1965 amendment to the MBA brought the criminal jurisdiction article in line with other SOFAs, and no further concessions were anticipated.

This review of several of the more serious substantive issues that remained unresolved at the conclusion of the working panel negotiations in August 1976 indicates that at least some of the accounts in the American press at the time were overly optimistic in reporting that progress was being made.[53] The fact is that the working panels had been successful in defining the respective positions of both countries on the issues but not in resolving or significantly narrowing the gap between these positions.

After a series of meetings in the fall between Kissinger and Romulo, the United States announced on December 4, 1976 that a tentative agreement had been reached. This settlement reportedly called for the U.S. to provide $1 billion to the Philippines over a five-year period, to be divided equally between economic and military assistance programs.[54] The following day, Marcos denied this report and stated that the compensation was not sufficient and that several of the issues raised by the working panels remained unresolved.[55]

For whatever reasons, the 1976 negotiations ended in failure. No solutions to some of the most vexing issues were reached, and the possibilities of an early resolution of the differences seemed even more remote as Gerald Ford was replaced by Jimmy Carter, who, as a presidential candidate, had indicated that respect for human rights would be a major determinant in selecting which countries would receive economic and military assistance from his administration.

The Carter administration's proposed Asian policies were outlined in testimony before the House Committee on International Relations in March 1977 by Assistant Secretary of State for East Asia-designate Richard Holbrooke.[56] Holbrooke's testimony served two purposes. The first was to reassure several Asian countries that the United States was not going to withdraw from the area, and the second was to attenuate domestic criticism over the decisions to reduce U.S. ground forces in Korea and normalize diplomatic relations with the PRC and possibly with Vietnam. All of these issues were controversial in the U.S. during this period. Specifically in regard to the Philippines, Holbrooke stated that the Carter administration looked forward to successful negotiations for the continued use of the military bases. In this manner and in the larger context of his testimony, Holbrooke viewed the base negotiations in much the same way as Kissinger, in that such negotiations provided tangible evidence that the United States would remain a regional power.

The negotiations that eventually would result in the very important 1979 amendment to the MBA began in September 1977.[57] The pertinent issues and respective positions of each country became clear as a result of a trip by Vice President Walter Mondale to the Philippines in May 1978. At the conclusion of this visit, Marcos and Mondale issued a Joint Statement that provided basic guidelines for the negotiations.[58] They agreed that the United States would respect Philippine sovereignty over the bases and that each base would be under the control of a Philippine Base Commander. However, the U.S. would be guaranteed effective "command and control over United States personnel, employees, equipment, material, and facilities authorized for their use within the military bases, and unhampered military operations involving their own forces." Finally, they stated that there would be a "thorough review and reassessment" of the MBA and its amendments every five years to ensure that the agreement continued to serve "the mutual interests of both parties." Marcos and Mondale in this statement set forth the guiding principles for the negotiations that once again revolved around the dilemma of trying to accommodate Philippine demands for the exercise of sovereignty over the bases with the U.S. insistence that unhampered military control over operations must remain with the United States.

Military officers from both countries conducted the actual negotiations from May to December 1978, when they concluded their work and submitted the amendment. President Marcos, in the effort to establish respect for Philippine sovereignty, identified three specific issues that became the heart of the discussions. These issues were: base land delimitation; the powers, duties, and responsibilities of the Philippine Base Commanders (PBCs); and perimeter security for the bases. All agreements were to be on an *ad referendum* basis, which meant they were subject to review and approval by higher authorities.[59]

A major impetus to these negotiations occurred in late October 1978 when Senator Daniel Inouye visited the Philippines. He was the Chairman of the Senate Appropriations Subcommittee on Foreign Operations and would play an important role in determining how much compensation the Philippines would receive for the bases. Marcos had raised the compensation issue repeatedly, which was impeding progress on the substantive issues under discussion. Inouye informed Marcos that he believed it was highly unlikely the Congress would approve an aid appropriation for the Philippines equal to that offered by Kissinger in December 1976 ($1 billion over five years). He stated that any aid program would face difficulties, but a supplemental appropriation would be even more difficult to pass. He recommended the negotiations be completed expeditiously so that any compensation could be included in the FY 1980 budget scheduled to be submitted to the Congress in January 1979.[60] Marcos apparently was impressed by Inouye's argument because the Philippine panel expressed new interest in reaching an accord, and the negotiations ended on December 26, 1978, with a tentative agreement reached on land delimitation, the duties and responsibilities of the PBCs, and base perimeter security.

Representatives of both countries signed this MBA amendment on January 7, 1979.[61] Because Clark Air Base and Subic Naval Base are the two most important bases in the Philippines, the land delimitation arrangements discussed here will be restricted to these two bases. In both cases, a U.S. facility was established within the much larger Philippine base. In actuality, the facilities contained most of the built-up areas and operational locations existing at the time the amendment was reached. However, the land returned to Philippine control was substantial. At Clark, over 119,000 acres of the original 130,000 acres reverted to the Philippines. At Subic, over 47,000 of the original 62,000 acres similarly reverted.[62]

Annex III of the 1979 amendment addressed the powers and responsibilities of the Philippine and American commanders on the bases and the facilities within the bases. In the performance of their duties, the respective commanders were to be guided by "full respect for Philippine sovereignty . . . and the assurance of unhampered United States military operations . . . " Close coordination and cooperation were stressed, if the amendment was to implemented successfully. The PBCs had the authority to "formulate and issue plans, policies, and implementing directives concerning security, maintenance of order and related matters applicable throughout the base."

These broad powers were tempered, however, by the provision that the PBCs had no authority over U.S. facilities, American personnel, dependents, or civilian employees unless the American commander of the particular facility approved. In effect, U.S. military officers had a veto over any plans or policies that affected American facilities or personnel assigned to them. Two new Philippine commands came into existence with this amendment: Clark Air Base Command (CABCOM) and Subic Naval Base Command (SUBCOM). These commands and their American counterparts were to be the primary consultative bodies in the implementation of the amendment provisions.

President Marcos indicated during the final stages of the negotiations in December 1978 that the assumption of the base security functions would be a major manifestation of Philippine sovereignty. The 1979 amendment provided that the PBCs were responsible for the overall security of the bases, and the U.S. commanders for the security of the American facilities within the bases. The PBCs were authorized to exercise control over the gates leading into and out of the bases in accordance with the security plans established through the cooperation of the commands involved.

These security responsibilities were important not only for the sovereignty issue, but also because having Filipinos on the gates and patrolling the base perimeters addressed a major complaint expressed since the early years of the MBA. American security guards apprehending Filipinos who violated base security often led to highly publicized disputes over criminal jurisdiction. This new procedure reduced the likelihood of these incidents being repeated. Fiscal constraints have limited Philippine assumption of perimeter security functions, but efforts continue to achieve that end.[63]

On compensation, President Carter sent a letter to President Marcos, delivered at the time of the amendment signing, that pledged his "best effort" to convince the Congress to appropriate the funds for the following assistance programs:

Military Assistance (MAP)—$50 million
Foreign Military Sales Credits—$250 million
Security Supporting Assistance—$200 million

In addition, Carter promised to give "sympathetic consideration" to Philippine requests for specific military equipment that the Philippines might want to purchase from the U.S. This appears to have been an effort to satisfy Marcos that the United States would assist his plans to achieve military self-sufficiency. In another letter from U.S. Ambassador Richard Murphy to Foreign Minister Romulo, the U.S. agreed to the five-year review of the MBA originally decided upon during the Mondale visit.

This amendment was criticized by several influential Filipinos, including former Senators Jovito Salonga and Jose Diokno. Salonga's criticism concentrated both on the substance of the amendment and its effects upon the continuation of martial law. He characterized the concessions made by the United States, such as the appointments of the PBCs, as being nothing more than symbolic. Salonga charged that as long as the U.S. retained the right of unhampered military operations, Philippine control over the bases would be extremely limited. He was critical of the $500 million compensation because he believed this contributed directly to Marcos remaining in power and continuing martial law.[64] Diokno's objections focused on broader issues similar to those of Claro Recto in the early postwar years. He stated that the U.S. military presence not only restricted Philippine sovereignty but also limited the necessary political and economic changes he felt were essential if the Philippines was to be a truly independent country. As long as the bases remained, the United States would continue to interfere in Philippine domestic politics and restrict the reforms Diokno believed were essential.[65]

President Marcos made a state visit to the United States in September 1982. In his discussions with President Ronald Reagan and other officials, they agreed to hold base negotiations beginning in April 1983.[66] Philippine Ambassador Benjamin Romualdez and U.S. Ambassador Michael Armacost conducted these negotiations between April 11 and June 1, 1983, when they reached agreement. The fact that the 1983 talks were much shorter in duration than those in 1979 is instructive in that the issues discussed apparently were not as contentious.[67]

The 1983 Review

As a result of the 1983 review, the United States did agree to increased consultations with the Philippines over military combat operations conducted from the bases, and a Military Bases Agreement Joint Committee was established to facilitate this consultation. However, it is clear that this agreement did not entail asking for permission from the Philippine government. In fact, the U.S. agreed to "inform" the Philippines of the current level of forces deployed and what equipment and weapons systems were in-country, and to "notify" the government of any major changes in either these forces and/or their weapons. In this manner, the amendment did reference Philippine sovereignty, but unhampered U.S. control over military operations remained relatively intact. The amendment did provide that the PBCs or their designated representatives would have increased access to U.S. facilities, except those highly sensitive areas such as cryptographic centers or locations where classified equipment or information was stored. No other reference was made to PBC duties and responsibilities.

President Reagan sent President Marcos a letter indicating he would make his "best effort" to obtain congressional appropriations for the Philippines in the sum of $900 million over a five-year period just as President Carter had done in 1979. This assistance was to be in the following categories and amounts:

Military Assistance (MAP)—$125 million
Foreign Military Sales Credits—$300 million
Economic Support Funds—$475 million

Although there were reports that the Marcos government initially wanted $1.5 billion in assistance, the $900 million in 1983 represented a healthy increase over the $500 million in 1979.[68]

Former Senator Diokno was critical of the 1983 amendment as he had been of the 1979 version. He raised the issue of nuclear weapons storage at the bases and the inherent dangers to the Philippines in case of war. He repeated his previous arguments that his country could never be truly sovereign as long as the bases remained.[69] Emmanuel Pelaez, who participated in the 1956 negotiations with Karl Bendetsen and is now Philippine Ambassador to the United States, voiced similar criticisms but also recommended that, if the bases remained, it would be the better course of action to write a new base agreement rather than continue to amend the original MBA.[70] U.S. support for Marcos' authoritarian regime also drew increased criticism from those opposed to that regime and to the presence of the bases.

Since the 1983 negotiations, cataclysmic events have occurred in the Philippines that will affect any future base discussions. The assassination of Benigno Aquino in August 1983, the precipitous decline of the Philippine political and economic systems in the aftermath of this assassination, and the "people power" revolution that forced Marcos from office and brought Corazon Aquino to the presidency are among the most important of these events. President Aquino has consistently taken the public position that she will abide by the terms of the MBA until its fixed term ends in 1991 and will keep her options open after that. The salient issue of base negotiations in the post-Marcos era, including consideration of the domestic Philippine political setting and new constitutional requirements, are discussed in the text.

In this review of postwar base negotiations, some conclusions are evident. First, there are very few new issues involved. Most of them have been raised and discussed in previous negotiations but not always resolved. Criminal jurisdiction, nuclear weapons, command and control, base land delimitation, base security, and compensation are among these recurring issues. Second, resolution of these issues is made more difficult because of the long-standing conflict between the need to respect Philippine sovereignty and the U.S. demand for continued unhampered control of military operations. Third, the historical relationship between the two countries exacerbates this tension to a certain extent because it gives additional credence to the arguments effectively made by nationalists such as former Senators Recto, Diokno, and others that the Philippines will never be an independent, sovereign country as long as the military bases remain.

Different threat perceptions also have affected and will continue to influence base negotiations. From the American perspective, the bases are extremely important in containing the increasing Soviet military presence in East Asia and in communicating the political intent of the United States to remain a regional power. For many Filipinos, the external threat from the Soviet Union or any other country is not considered to be imminent. The more serious threat is the internal security problem, particularly the MNLF and NPA insurgencies. For those identifying the threat in this manner, the value of the bases is that, beyond the training, equipment, and intelligence support provided through military aid, their continuation is a major boost to the Philippine economy, which helps address some of the political and economic causes of these insurgencies. Further, the bases are important to the Philippines because, in many ways, they are central to the political relationship between the two countries. Roxas understood this in 1946–1947, and he was correct in his evaluation that the bases keep the United States interested in events occurring in the Philippines. While some critics have argued that this close interest is inimical to Philippine independence and sovereignty, many other Filipinos support the retention of the bases because of it.

There is another factor that is hard to evaluate, but will likely influence the next negotiations. As a result of the "people power" revolution in February 1986, Filipinos feel good about themselves; they were able to rid themselves of an unpopular regime and install a very popular president in its place. This more profound sense of national pride must be appreciated. It will be in the best interest of the United States if future American negotiators not only understand the history of the issues involved, but also recognize the differences in threat perception and are familiar with the expectations the Philippine leaders and public have about the value of the bases to their country and to the region at this particular time in their history.

Colonel William E. Berry, Jr., is a career Air Force officer with assignments in Vietnam, the Philippines, and Korea. He has also served on the faculty of the USAF Academy and the National War College. Colonel Berry holds a Ph.D. from Cornell University and is the author of, among other works, "U.S. Security Policy in Asia," *in* American Defense Policy *(Johns Hopkins University Press, forthcoming.)*

Notes

1. *U.S. Statutes at Large,* Philippine Trade Act, Vol. 60 (1946), p. 14.
2. For Resident Commissioner Carlos Romulo's evaluation, see Shirley Jenkins, *American Economic Policy Toward the Philippines,* (Stanford: Stanford University Press, 1954), p. 63.
3. *U.S. Statutes at Large,* Philippine Rehabilitation Act, Vol. 60 (1946), p. 128.
4. Milton W. Meyer, *A Diplomatic History of the Philippine Republic,* (Honolulu: The University of Honolulu Press, 1965), p. 53.

5. *Foreign Relations of the United States, 1946*, Vol. VIII, pp. 921–922.
6. *New York Times* (*NYT*), November 18, 1946, p. 1.
7. *Ibid.*, p. 1.
8. *Foreign Relations of the United States, 1946*, Vol. VIII, pp. 934–935.
9. *Ibid.*, p. 934.
10. *Ibid.*, p. 935.
11. *Ibid.*, pp. 536–537.
12. Roxas' position is included in *U.S. High Commissioner to the Philippines*, "Seventh and Final Report of the High Commissioner to the Philippines Covering the Period from September 14, 1945 to July 4, 1946", dated July 8, 1947, p. 76.
13. Joint Resolution No. 4 can be found in *Philippine Official Gazette*, 349 (1945).
14. For details on the Osmena negotiations, see William E. Berry, Jr., *American Military Bases in the Philippines, Base Negotiations, and Philippine–American Relations: Past,, Present, and Future*, Unpublished Ph.D. Dissertation, Cornell University, 1981, pp. 131–136.
15. *Foreign Relations of the United States, 1946*, Vol. VIII, pp. 939–940.
16. *Foreign Relations of the United States, 1947*, Vol. VIII, pp. 1102–1103.
17. For one of the best examples of Philippine objections to exclusive jurisdiction, see the opinion of Justice Gregorio Perfecto in 78 *Philippine Reports* 249 (1947).
18. *Foreign Relations of the United States, 1946*, Vol. VIII, p. 917.
19. "Agreement Between the United States of America and the Republic of the Philippines Concerning Military Bases", 14 March 1947 in *Treaties and Other International Agreements Series* (hereafter TIAS) 1775 (1947–1948).
20. For such detail, see Berry, *op. cit.*, pp. 162–184.
21. Meyer, *op. cit.*, p. 47.
22. *Republic of the Philippines Congressional Record*, Senate, 1st Congress, Vol. II, No. 23, January–May 1947, pp. 215–216.
23. A copy of the NATO SOFA is available in *TIAS* 2846 (1954). For the Japanese agreements, see *TIAS* 2491 (1952–1954), *TIAS* 2492(1952–1954), and *TIAS* 2848 (1954).
24. *Department of State Bulletin*, Vol. XXII, No. 551, January 23, 1950, pp. 111–118.
25. *TIAS* 2529 (1952–1953).
26. *NYT*, March 15, 1954, p. 3.
27. Roberto Paterno, "American Military Bases in the Philippines: The Brownell Opinion", *Philippine Studies* Vol. 12, No. 3; July 1964, pp. 394–395.
28. *American Foreign Policy Current Documents 1956*, pp. 858–859.
29. *Philippine Free Press*, February 13, 1965, p. 12.
30. George E. Taylor, "The Challenge of Mutual Security," in *The United States and The Philippines*, (Englewood Cliffs, NJ: Prentice Hall, 1966), edited by Frank H. Golay, p. 88. See also *NYT*, August 14, 1956, p. 8.

31. *Philippine Free Press,* October 27, 1956, p. 2.
32. *NYT,* September 4, 1956, p. 10.
33. Author's interview with David T. Sternberg, September 8, 1979, in Manila. Sternberg was a close associate of Bohlen during this period.
34. *TIAS* 4033 (1958).
35. "Historical Report," July 1–December 31, 1958, p. 159, maintained in the 13th Air Force Office of History, Clark Air Base, Republic of the Philippines.
36. Memorandum of Agreements (Bohlen–Serrano Agreement), October 12, 1959. A copy of this agreement is found in "U.S. Security Agreements and Commitments Abroad: The Republic of the Philippines," Hearings before the Committee on Foreign Relations, U.S. Senate 91st Congress, 1st Session, October 30, 1969, pp. 24–25.
37. *Department of State Bulletin,* Vol. 55, No. 1424, October 10, 1966, pp. 547–548.
38. *American Foreign Policy Current Documents 1958,* pp. 1249–1251.
40. A copy of the Marino Report is located in *Philippine International Law Journal,* Vol. 3, Nos. 3–4, July–December 1964, pp. 535–550.
41. *Philippine Free Press,* February 13, 1965, p. 12.
42. *NYT,* February 5, 1965, p. 2.
43. *TIAS,* 5851 (1965).
44. *TIAS,* 5051 (1965).
45. *Philippine Official Gazette,* Vol. 71, No. 17, April 28, 1975, pp. 2420–2431.
46. Joint Communique of President Marcos and President Ford, December 1, 1975 (author's copy).
47. *Department of State Bulletin,* Vol. LXXV, No 1938, August 16, 1976, pp. 217–226.
48. "The USAF Role in the U.S.–RP Negotiations 1976–1979", p. 2. This report was compiled by Robert F. Johnston, II, who was closely associated with the negotiations as an advisor to the 13th Air Force Commander. This report is hereafter referred to as the Johnston Report.
49. "Summary Record of U.S./R.P. Negotiations–December 7, 1975 to 1979." This is a document outlining the negotiations at the request of both the Philippine and American negotiating teams. It is hereafter referred to as the *Summary Record.*
50. *Ibid.,* Document s6.
51. *Ibid.,* Document s6.
52. *Ibid.,* Document s6.
53. *NYT,* October 31, 1976, p. 14.
54. *NYT,* December 4, 1976, p. 1.
55. *NYT,* December 5, 1976, p. 1.
56. *Department of State Bulletin,* Vol. LXXVI, No. 1971, April 4, 1977, pp. 322–326.
57. For a full account of these negotiations, see Berry, *op. cit.,* pp. 314–358.

58. Joint Statement of President Marcos and Vice President Mondale, May 4, 1978 in *TIAS* 9224 (1979), p. 6.
59. *Summary Record, op. cit.,* p. 18.
60. *Johnston Report, op. cit.,* p. 18.
61. *TIAS,* 9224 (1979).
62. Berry, *op. cit.,* pp. 360–362.
63. During a visit to Clark Air Base in April 1987, both Philippine and American officials discussed some of the problems involved with security with the author. They cited the lack of adequate funds as a major reason the Philippines has not been able to do as much as it would like to provide for base security.
64. *Philippine Times,* March 24–30, 1979, p. 5.
65. Author's interview with Jose W. Diokno, September 14, 1979 in Manila.
66. *NYT,* February 27, 1982, p. 8 and *Far Eastern Economic Review* (hereafter *FEER*), September 24–30, 1982.
67. For a copy of the 1983 MBA Amendment and related documents, see *Foreign Relations Journal,* a publication of the Philippine Council for Foreign Relations, Vol. 1, No. 1, January 1986, pp. 200–214.
68. *FEER,* May 19, 1983, pp. 40–41.
69. *Ibid.,* pp. 40–41 and *FEER,* June 16, 1983, pp. 30–32.
70. Emmanuel Pelaez, "The Military Bases in the Philippines: The Past and Future", *Foreign Relations Journal,* Vol. 1, No. 1, January 1986, pp. 27–28.

Council on Foreign Relations Study Group on U.S.–Philippine Bases Agreement: Looking to the Future

Participants

Brent Scowcroft (Co-Chairman)	Kissinger Associates
Theodore L. Eliot, Jr. (Co-Chairman)	The Asia Foundation Center for Asian Pacific Affairs
John J. Bresnan	Columbia University
William P. Bundy	Princeton University
Peter M. Flanigan	Dillon, Read & Co.
S. R. Foley, Jr.	Foley Associates, Inc.
William H. Gleysteen, Jr.	Council on Foreign Relations
Fred Greene	Williams College
Thomas B. Hayward	Thomas B. Hayward Associates
Stanley Karnow	Author and Journalist
Paul H. Kreisberg	Carnegie Council for International Peace
Herbert Levin	The Asia Foundation Center for Asian Pacific Affairs
David E. McGiffert	Covington & Burling
David D. Newsom	Georgetown University
Alan D. Romberg	Council on Foreign Relations
Paul S. Slawson	Inter-Pacific, Inc.
Robert Shaplen	*The New Yorker*
W. Y. Smith	Institute of Defense Analyses
David J. Steinberg	Long Island University
George K. Tanham	The Rand Corporation
Peter Tarnoff	Council on Foreign Relations
Mitzi M. Wertheim	IBM Corporation
Richard W. Wheeler	The Bank of the Philippine Islands
Casimir A. Yost	World Affairs Council of Northern California

Participants at the Bodega Bay Conference

John J. Bresnan
Jorge P. Coquia
Jose Mario C. Cuyegkang
Theodore L. Eliot, Jr. (*Absent due to illness*)
Enrique P. Esteban
Florentino P. Feliciano
S. R. Foley, Jr.
William H. Gleysteen, Jr.
Fred Greene
Thomas B. Hayward
Carolina G. Hernandez
Maria Elena Chiong-Javier
Pilar Ramos-Jimenez
Paul H. Kreisberg
Herbert Levin
Jose P. Leviste, Jr.
David E. McGiffert

Estelito P. Mendoza
David D. Newsom
Wilhelm G. Ortaliz
Rudolph A. Peterson
Purificacion V. Quisumbing
Alan D. Romberg
Bonifacio S. Salamanca
Brent Scowcroft
Paul Slawson
W. Y. Smith
Estrella D. Solidum
Enrique P. Syquia
Pablo Tangco
Peter Tarnoff
Cesar E. A. Virata
Mitzi M. Wertheim
Richard W. Wheeler